Vol. 1

Nightscapes

art by
Hamid Molavi

Copyright © – 2022 – Hamid Molavi
All cover art and interior artwork copyright © – 2022 – Hamid Molavi
All Rights Reserved

No part of this book may be reproduced or transmitted in any form or by any means, electronic or mechanical, including photocopying, recording, or by any information storage and retrieval system, without permission in writing from the author.

Publishing Coordinator – Sharon Kizziah-Holmes

Paperback-Press
an imprint of A & S Publishing
Paperback Press, LLC

ISBN -13: 978-1-956806-76-2

Acknowledgments

First, I'd like to thank the Lord for giving me the gift of sketching/drawing.

To my mother, Pouran, thank you for your unconditional love and support of my projects throughout my life.

Thanks to my brother and sister, Alex and Pantea, for their appreciation of my artworks and for encouraging me to pursue my goals and talents.

Next, I like to thank my coworkers for their support of my work.

Last but not least, thanks to my publishing coordinator Sharon. Without your help this project would have never been completed.

"Every gift is from above" -Holy Bible.

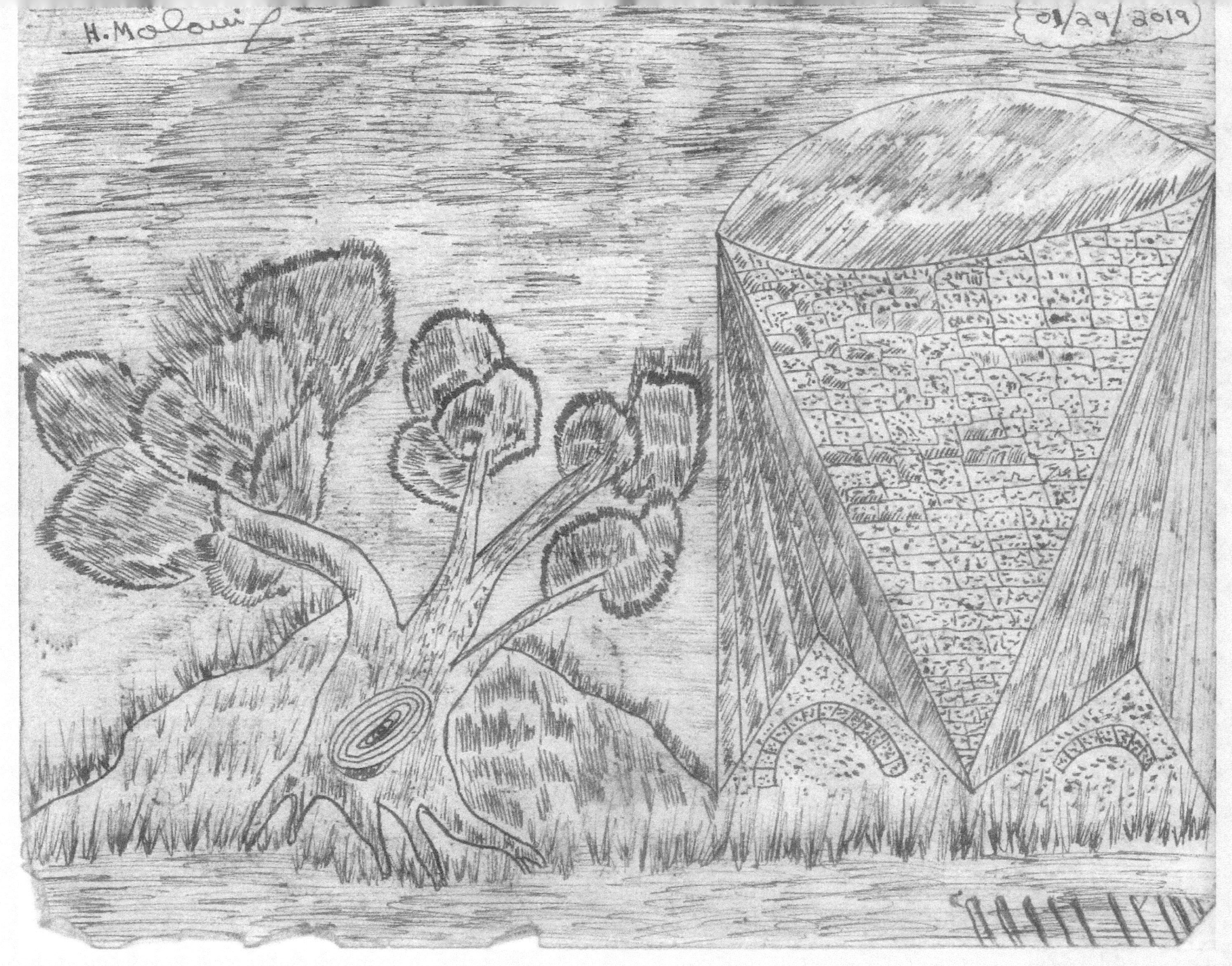

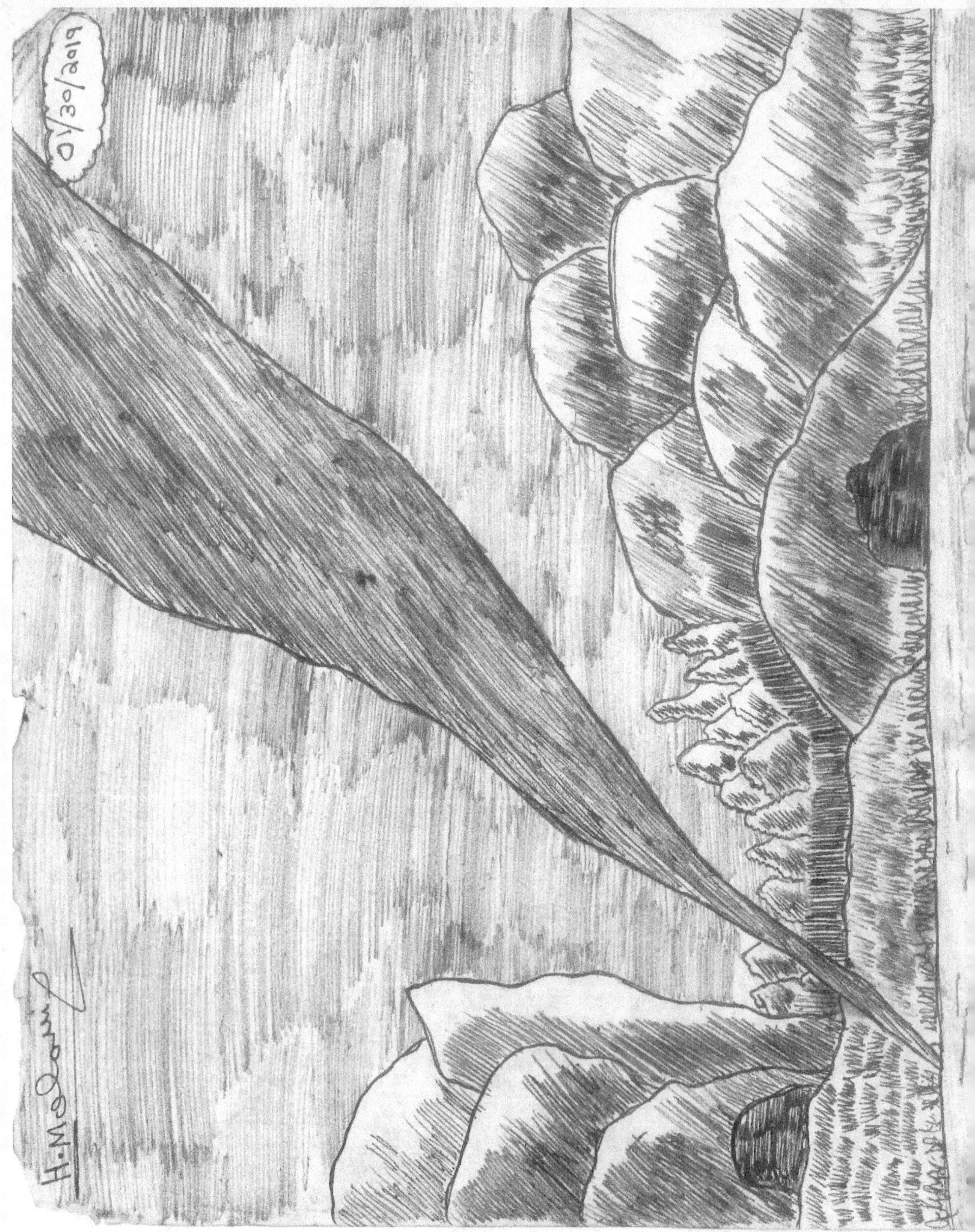

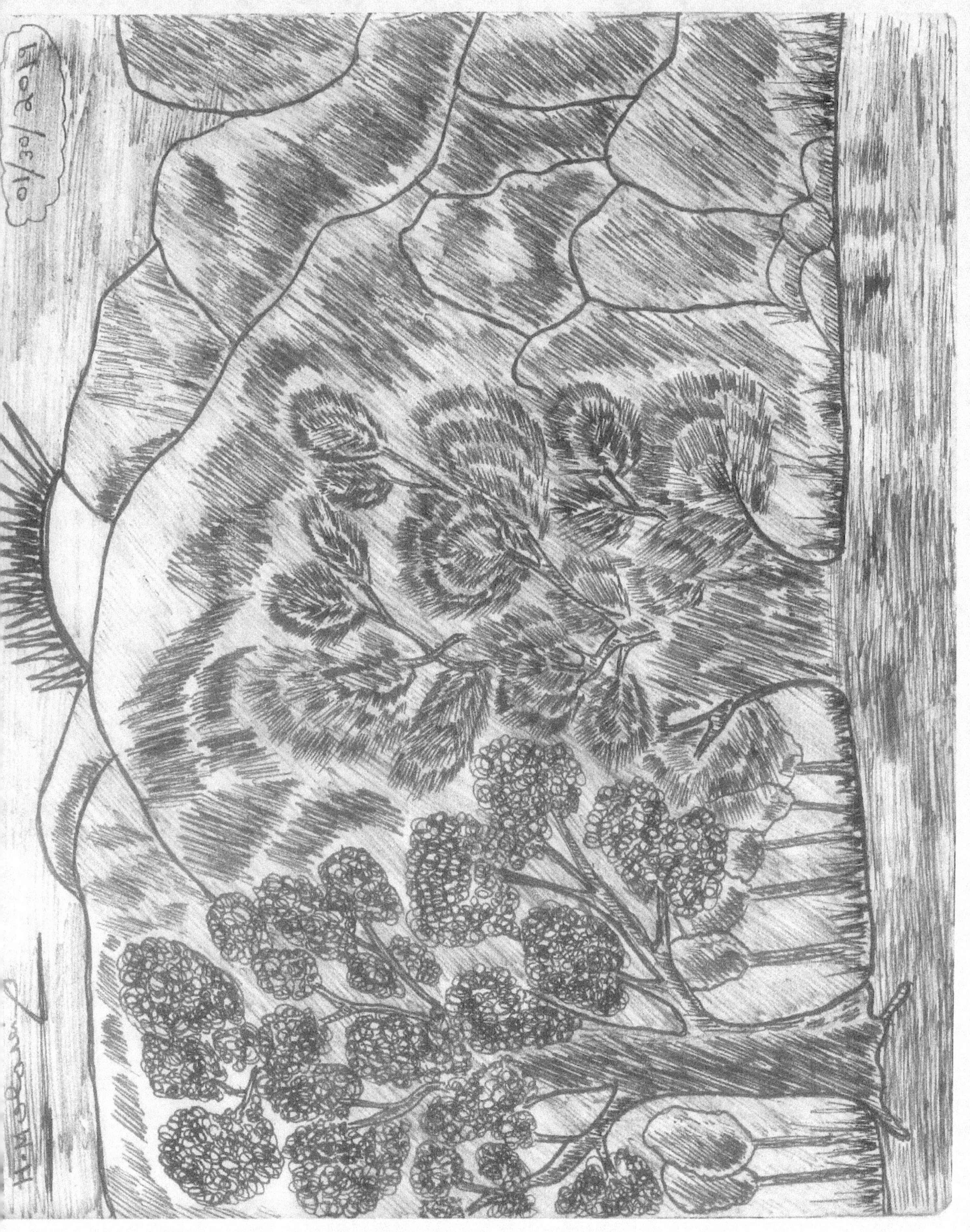

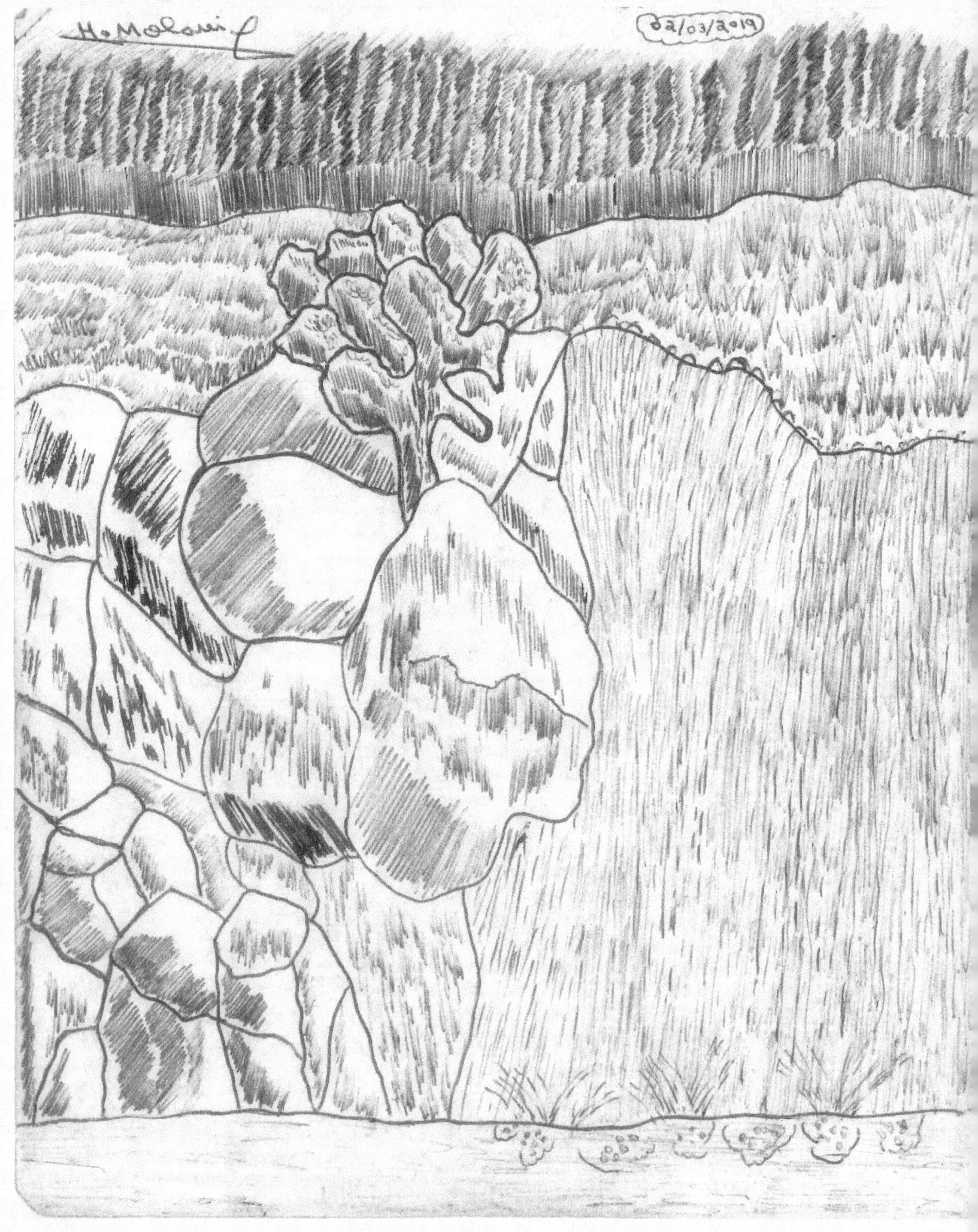

H. Molani
02/03/2019

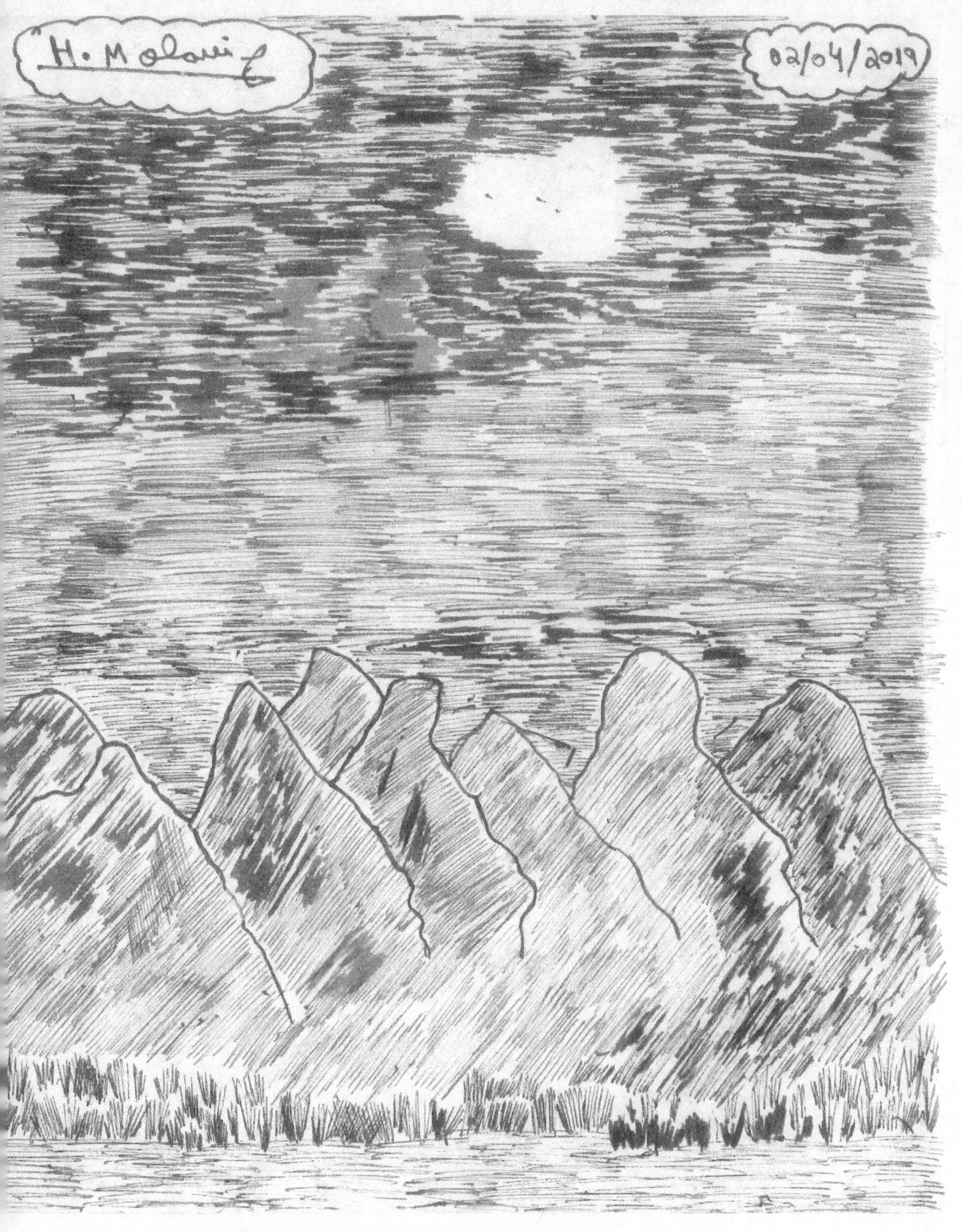

H. Molani
02/04/2019

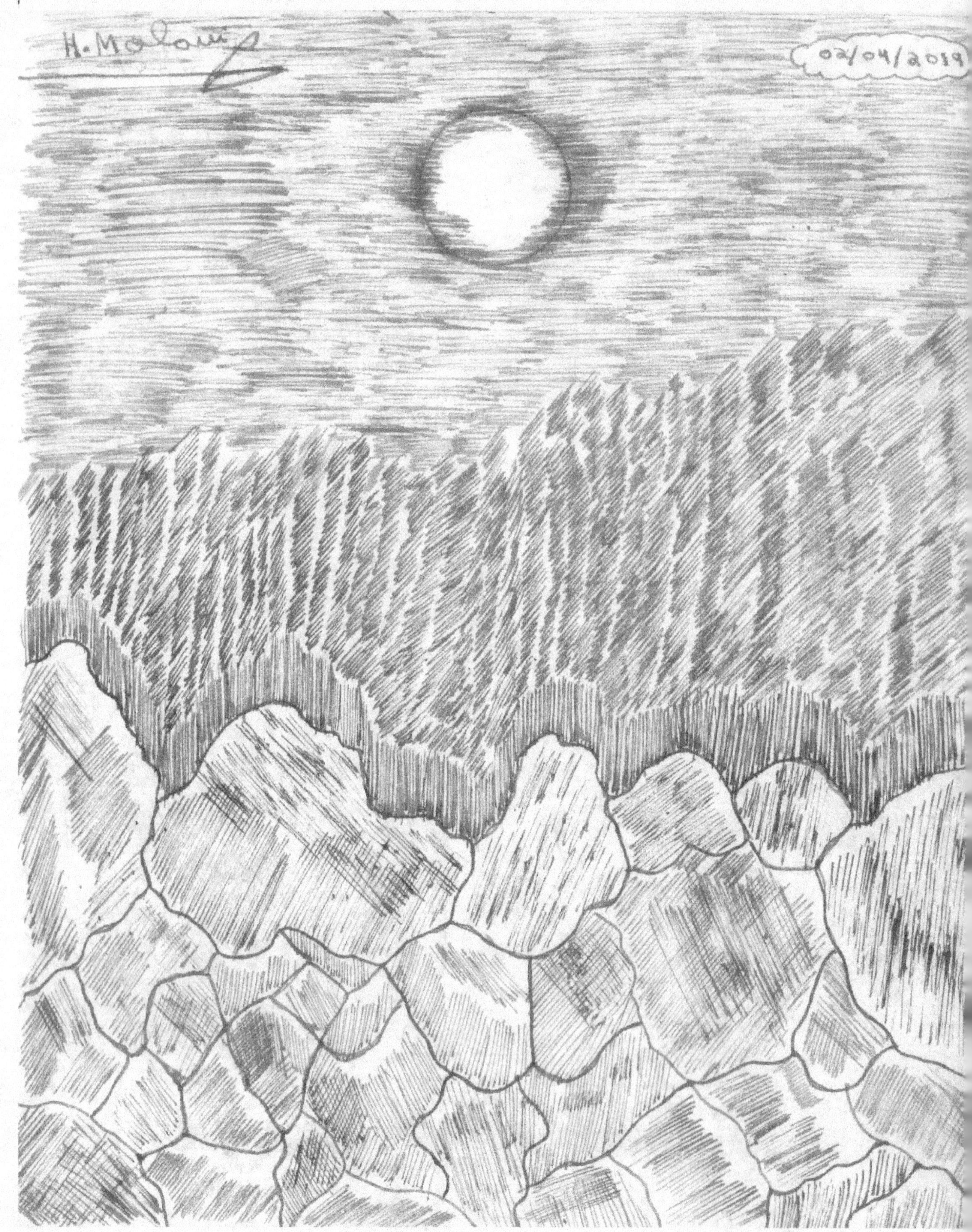

H. Malaui
02/04/2019

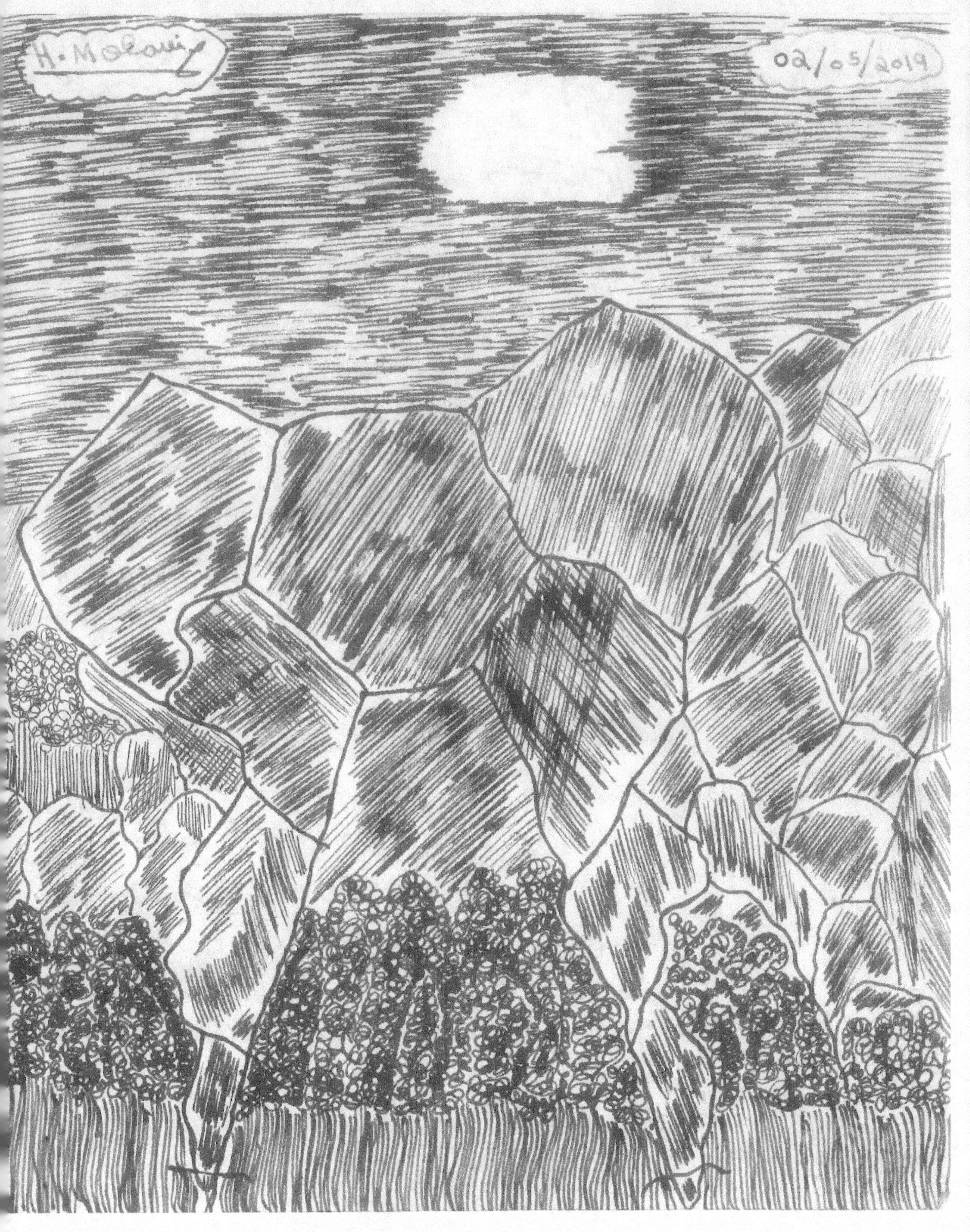
H. Molaui
02/05/2019

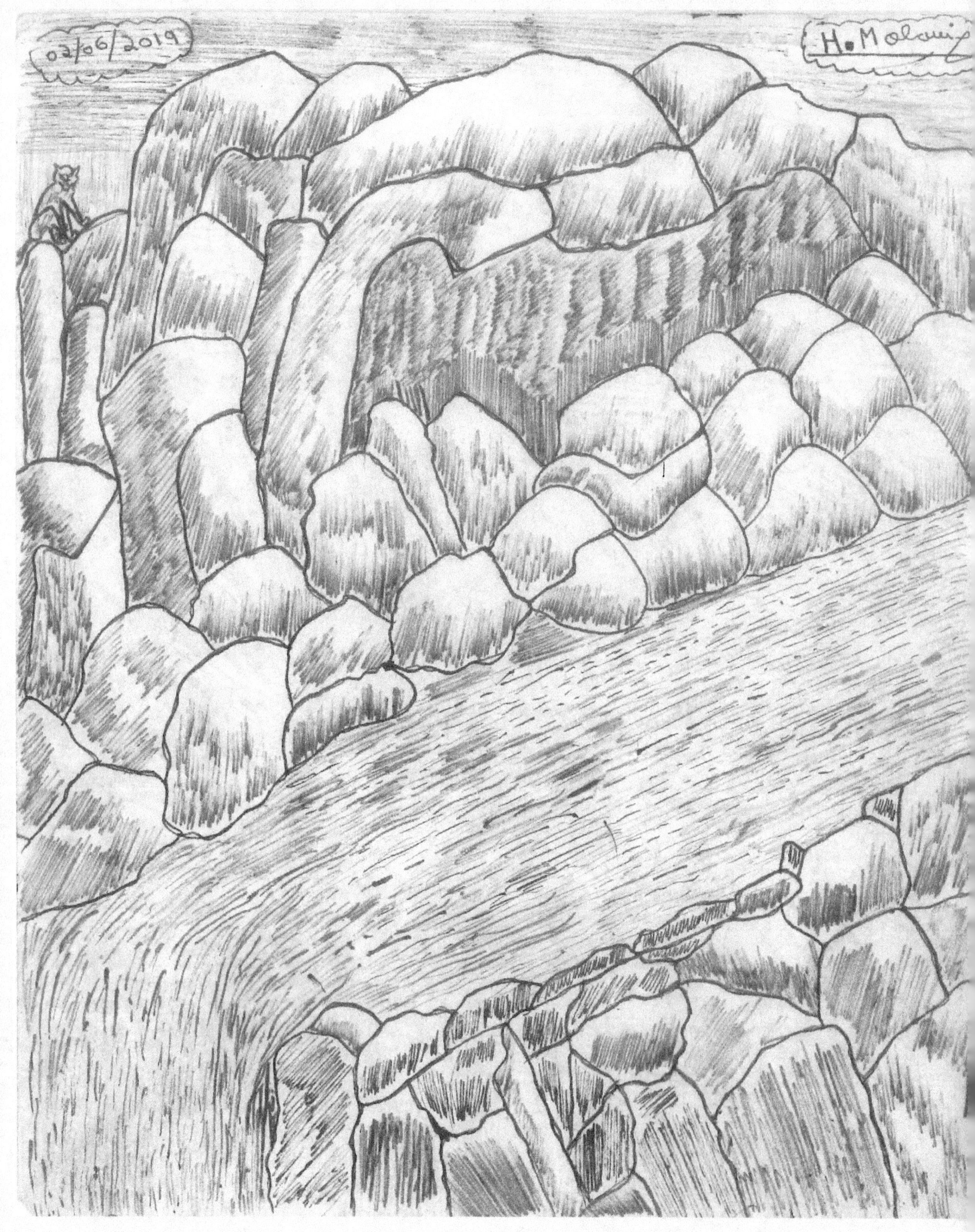

02/06/2019
H. Molaui

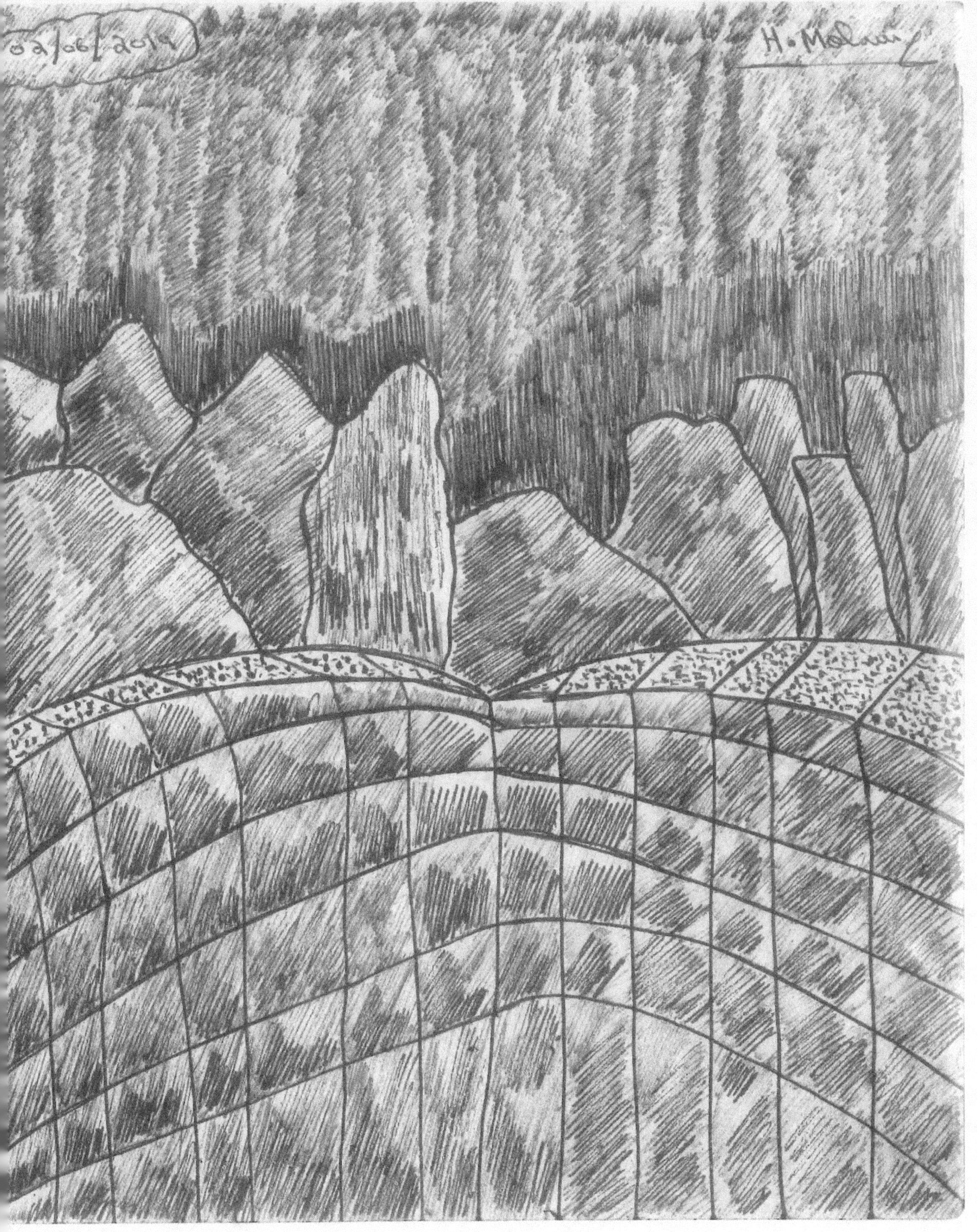

02/06/2019
H. Molnar

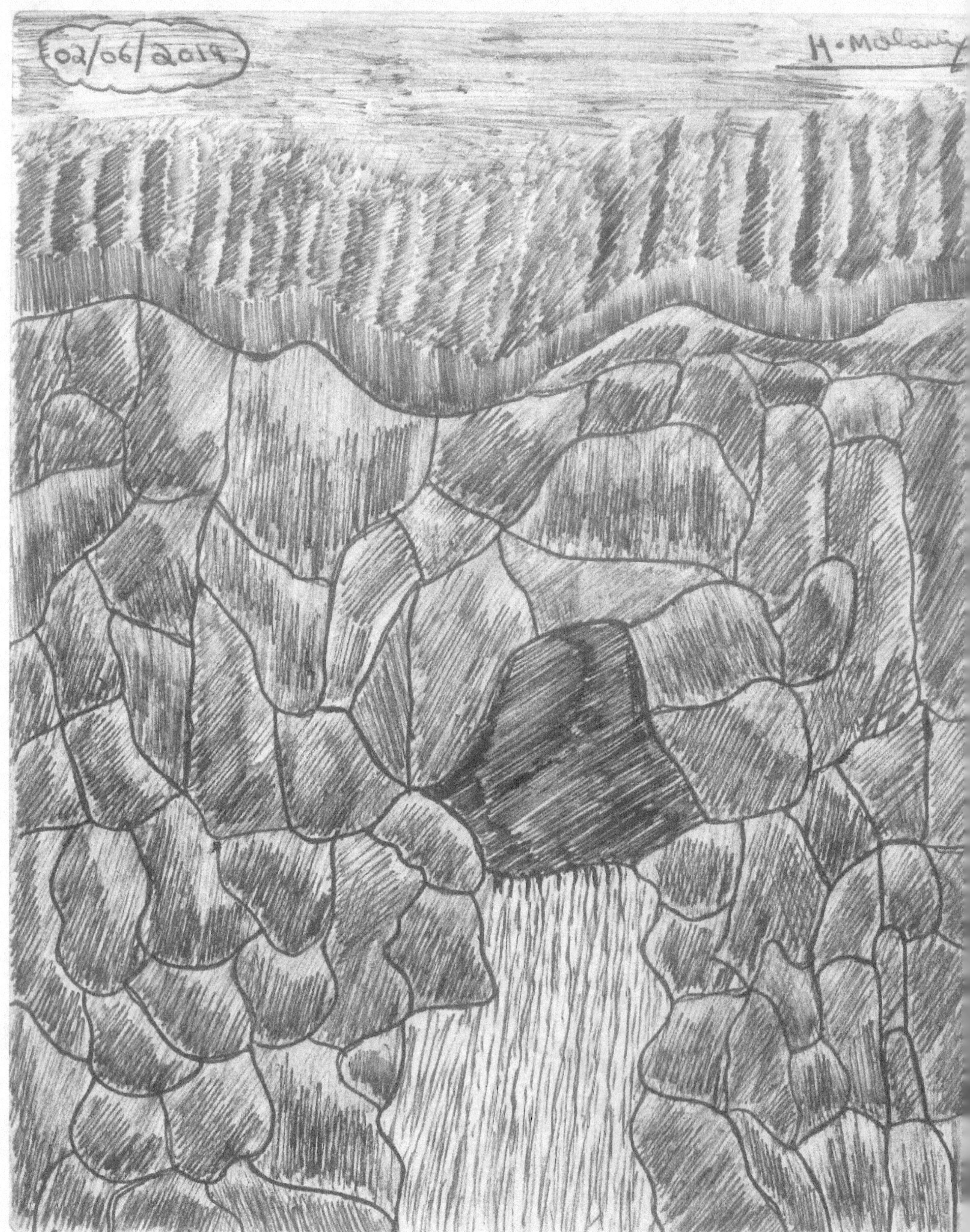

02/06/2019
H. Mólaui

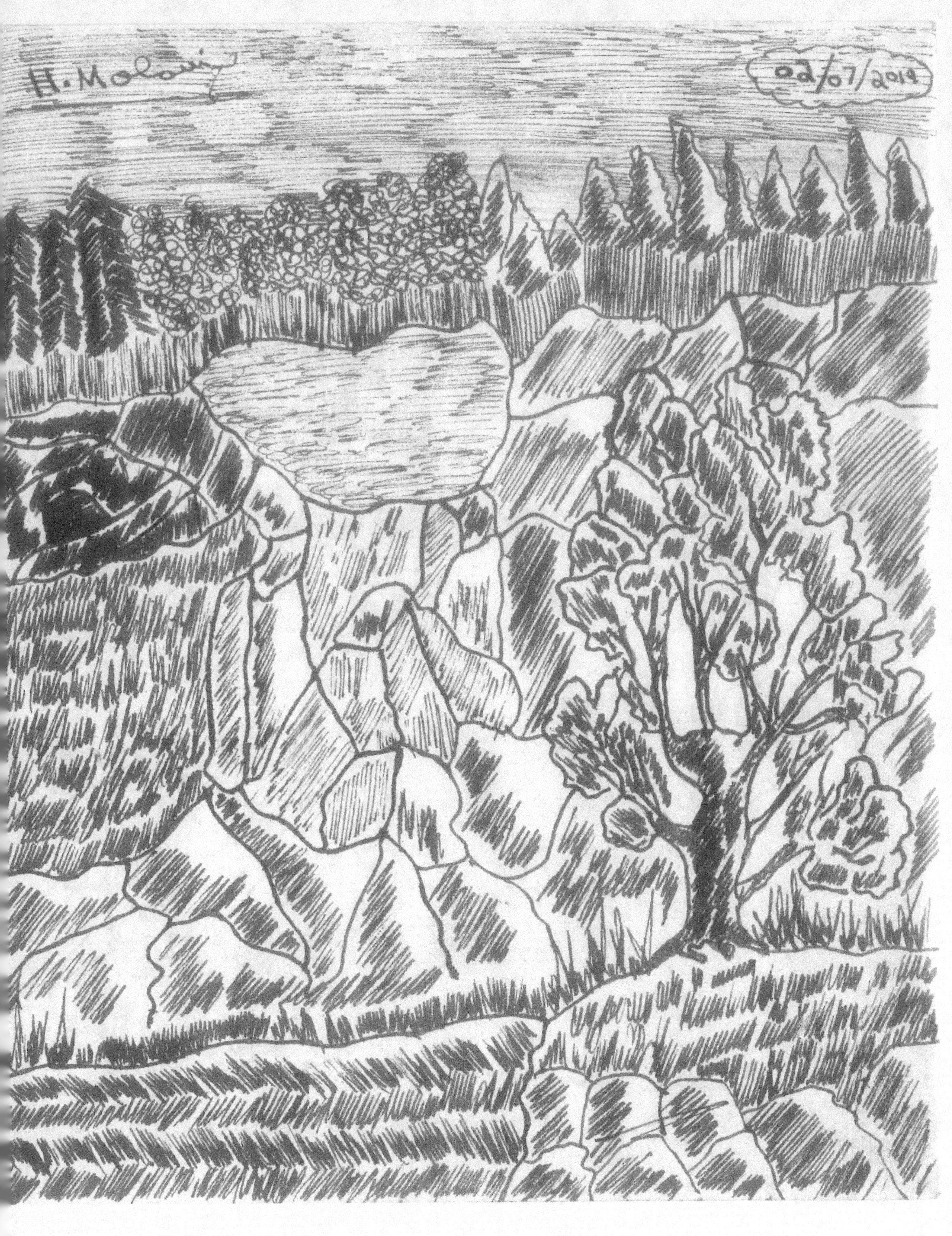

H. Molo...
02/07/2019

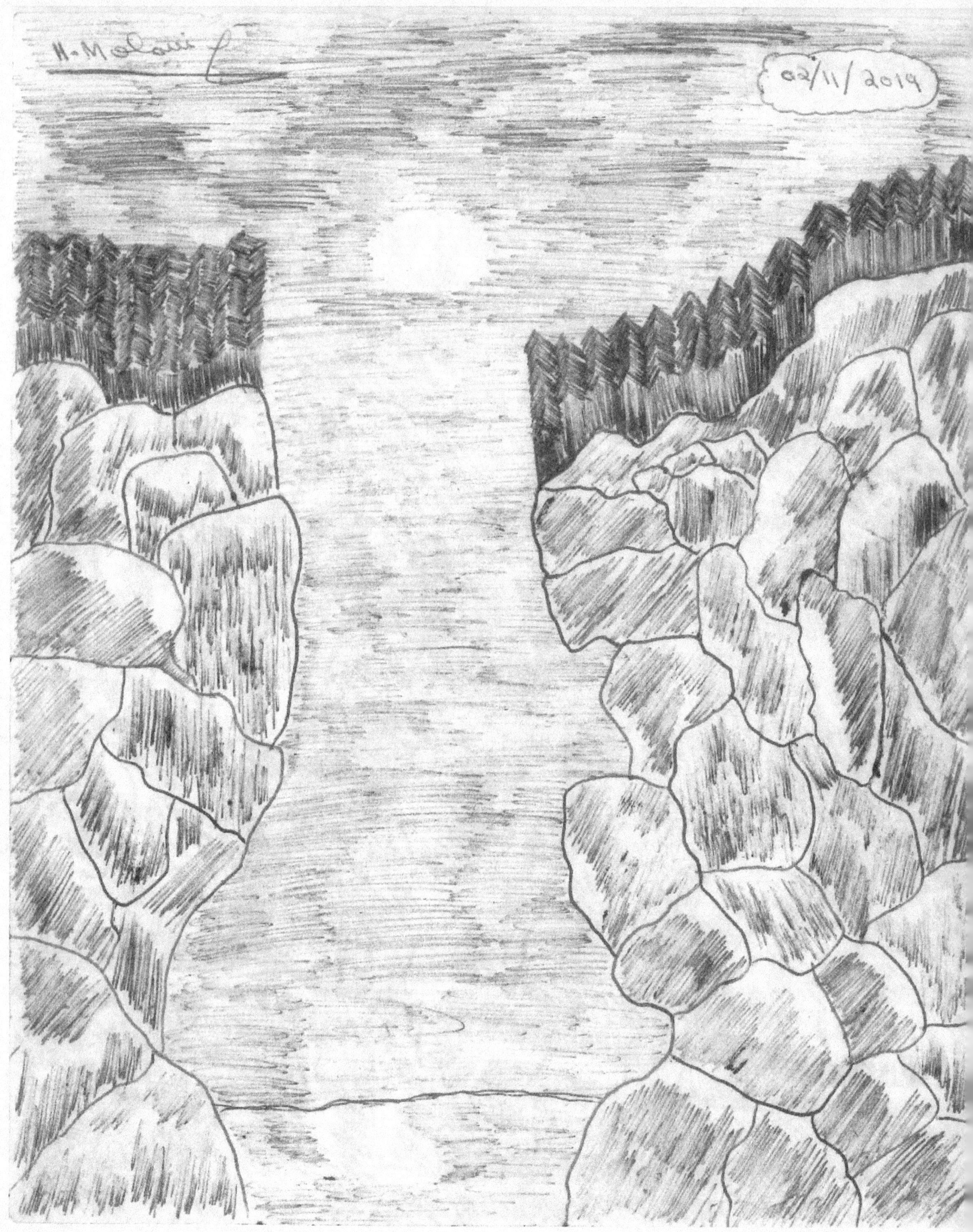
H. Molaii
02/11/2019

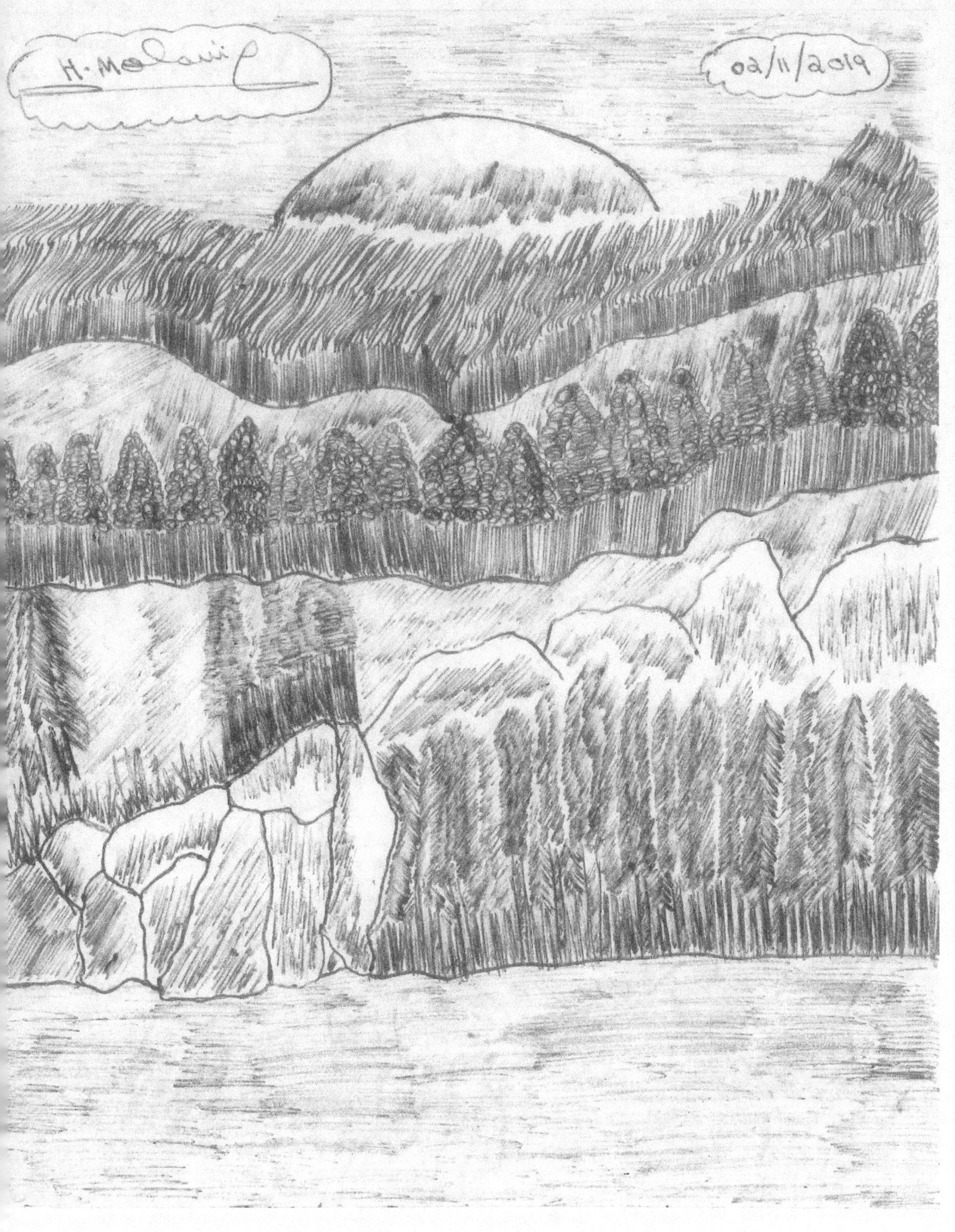

H. Melani
02/11/2019

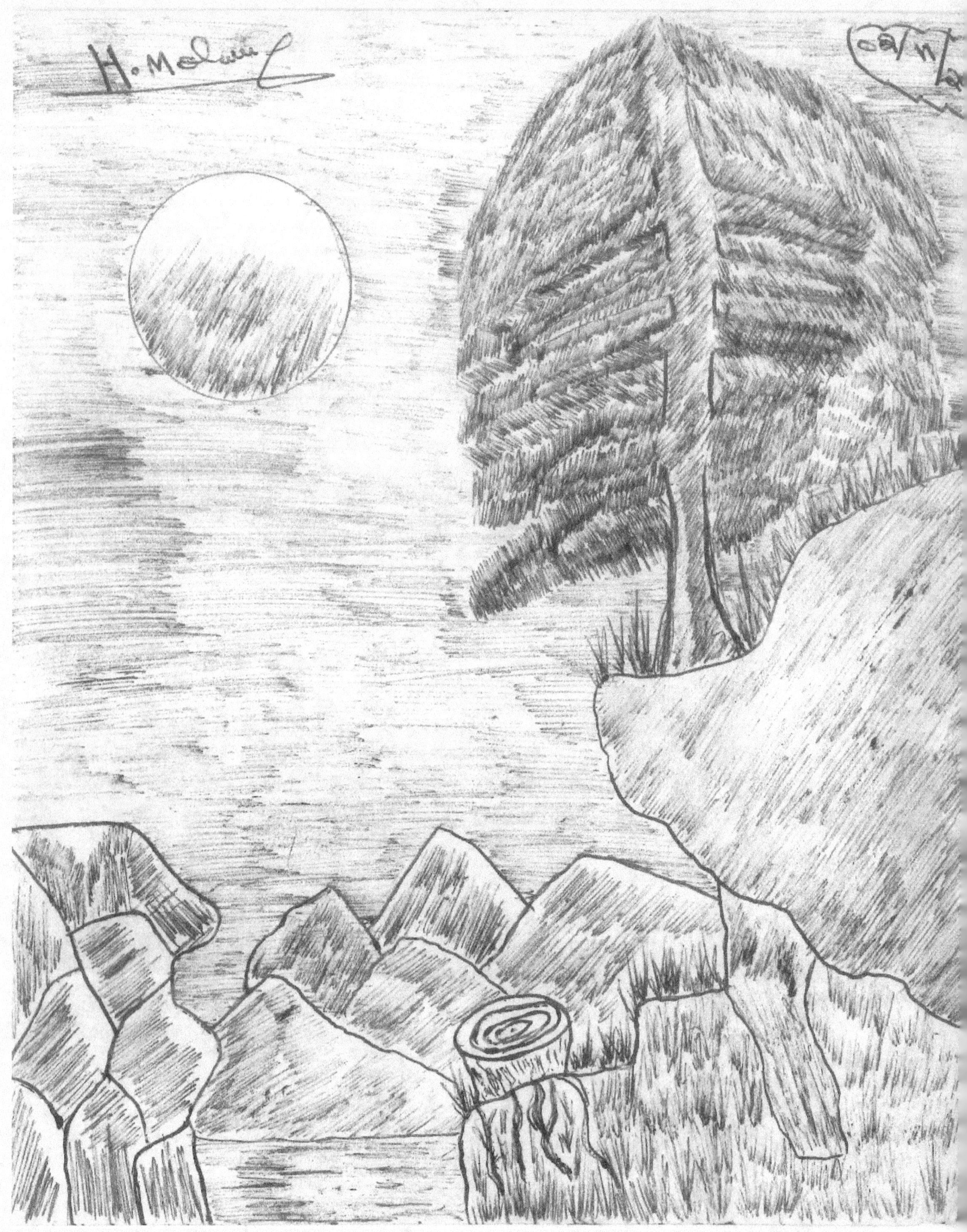

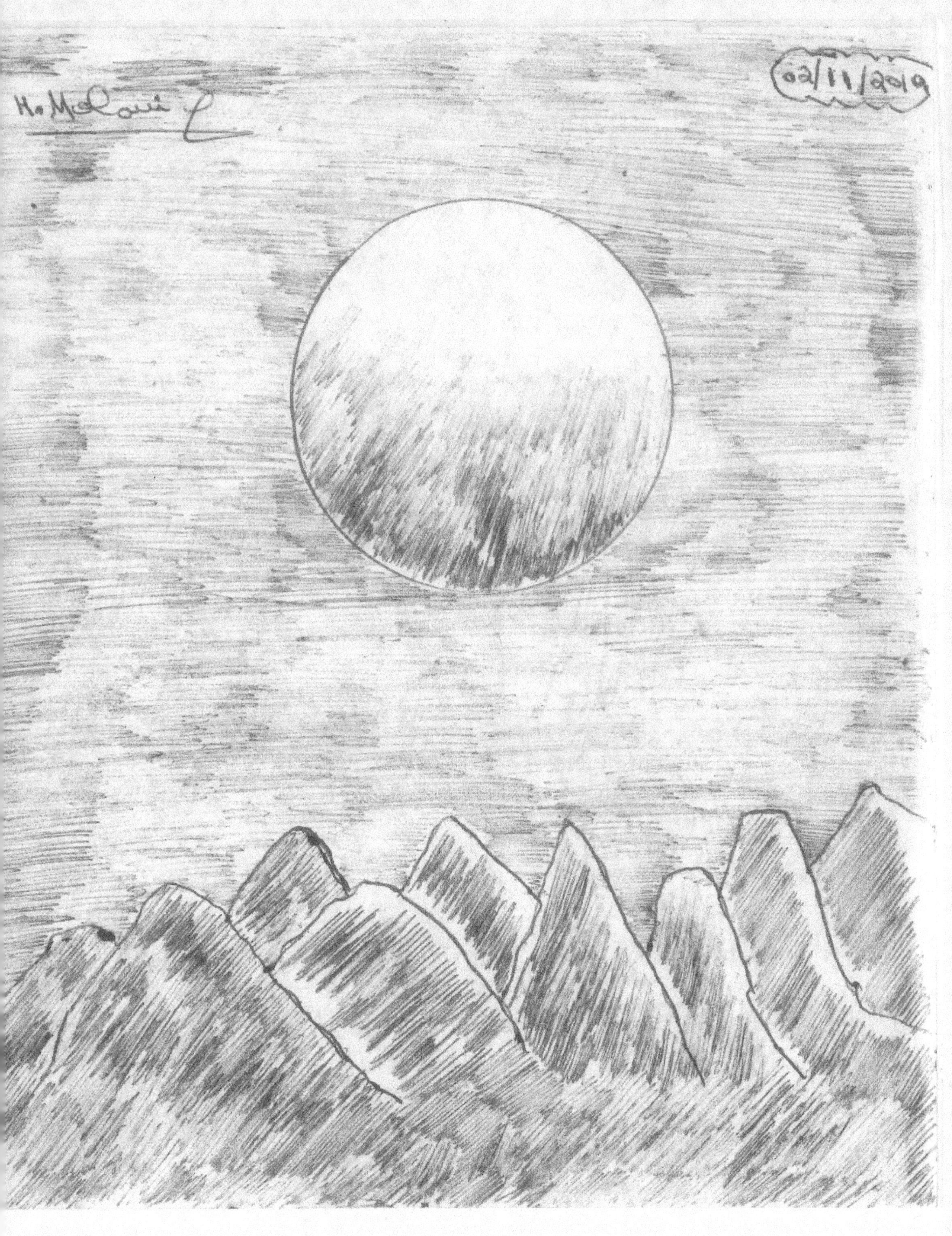

02/11/2019

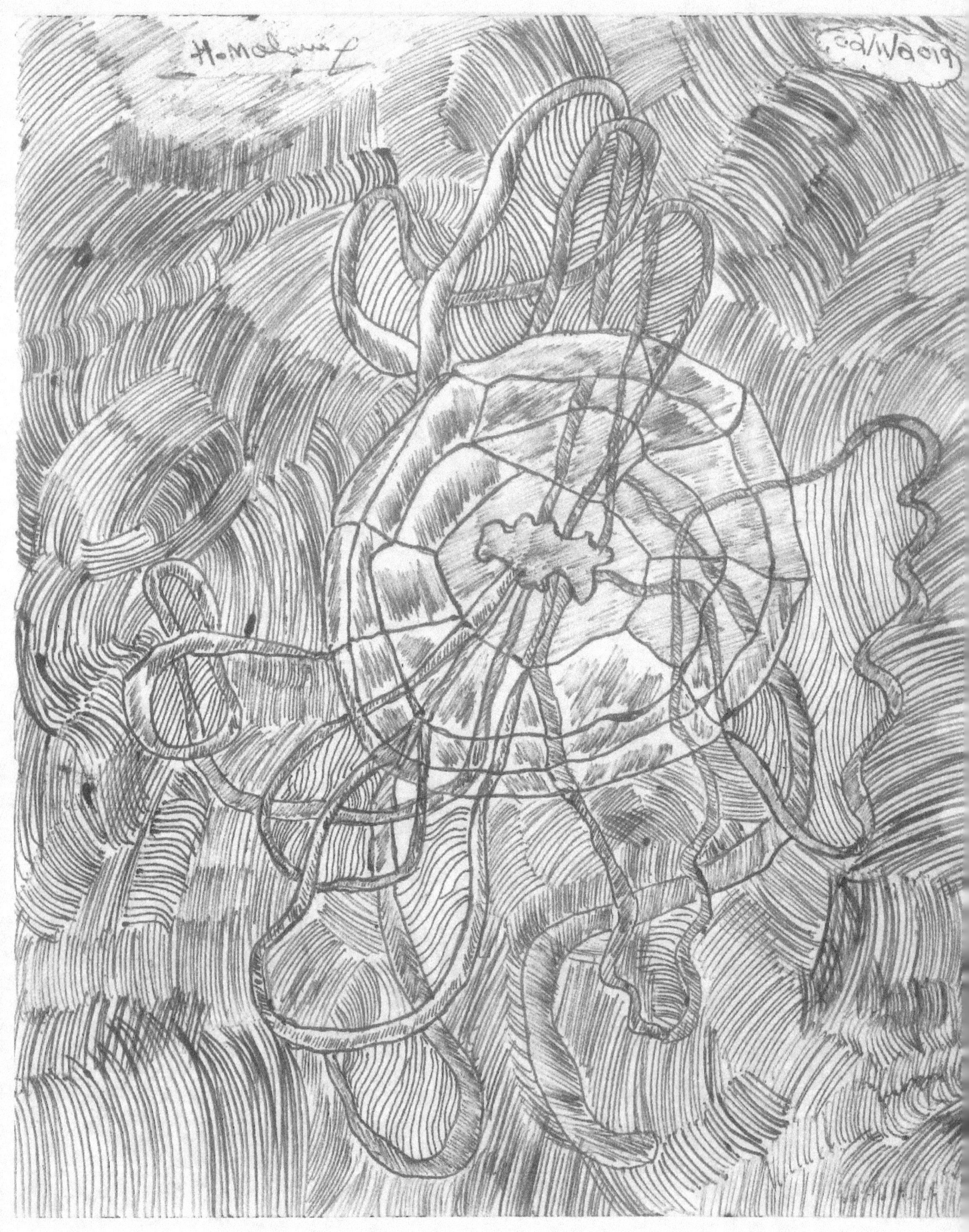

Homalauf
02/11/2019

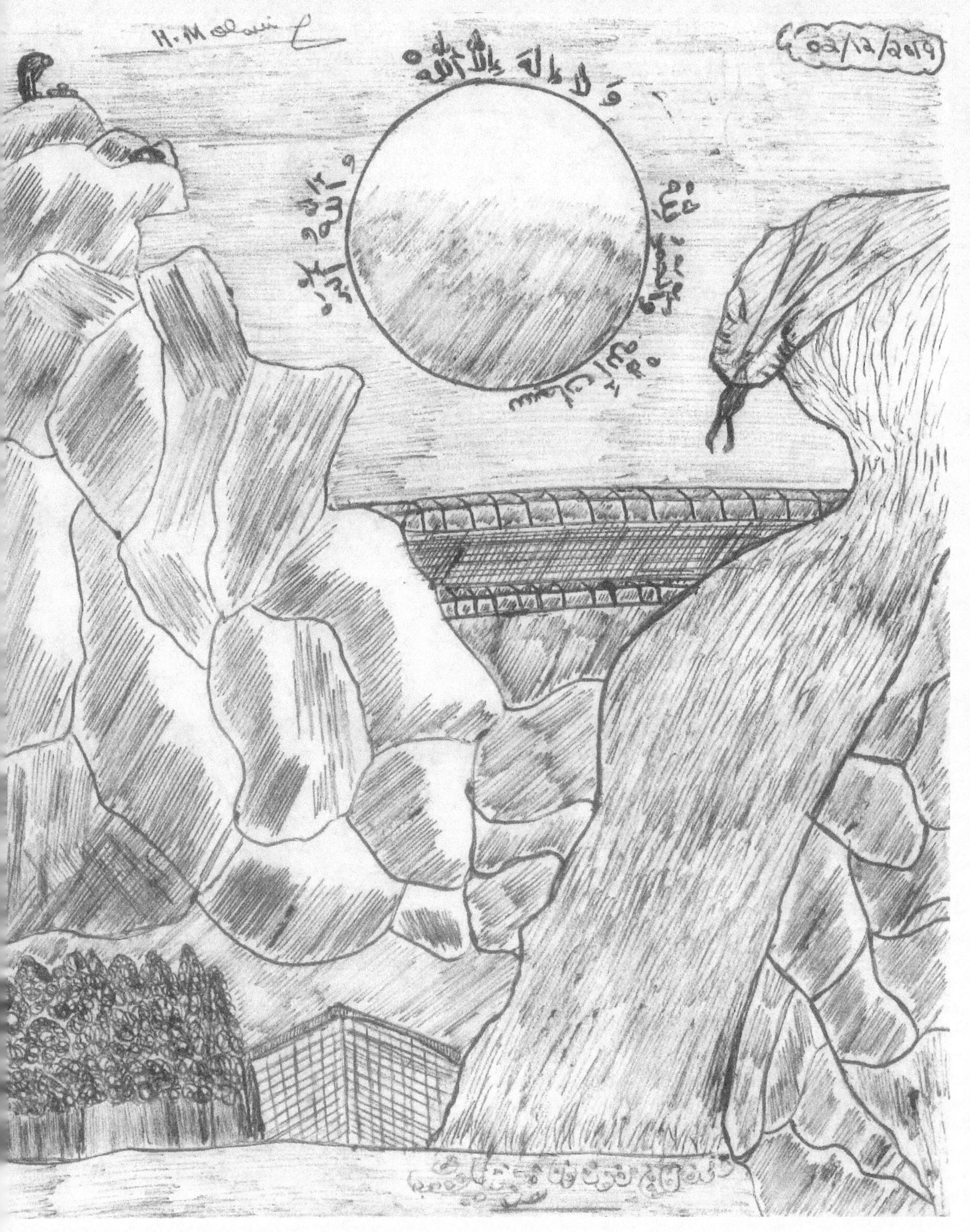

H. Molaie
٠٢/١٢/٢٠١٩

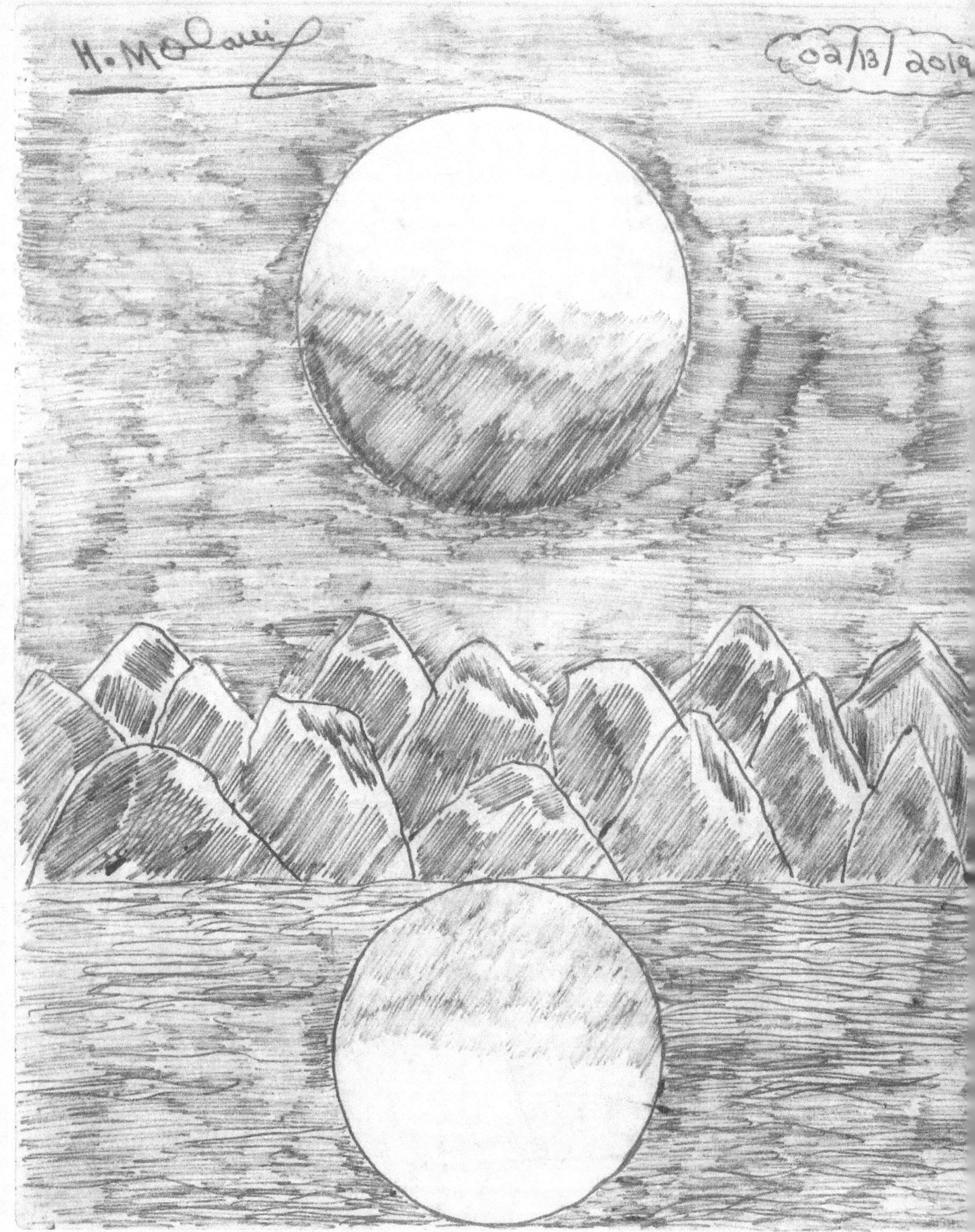

H. Molani
02/13/ 2019

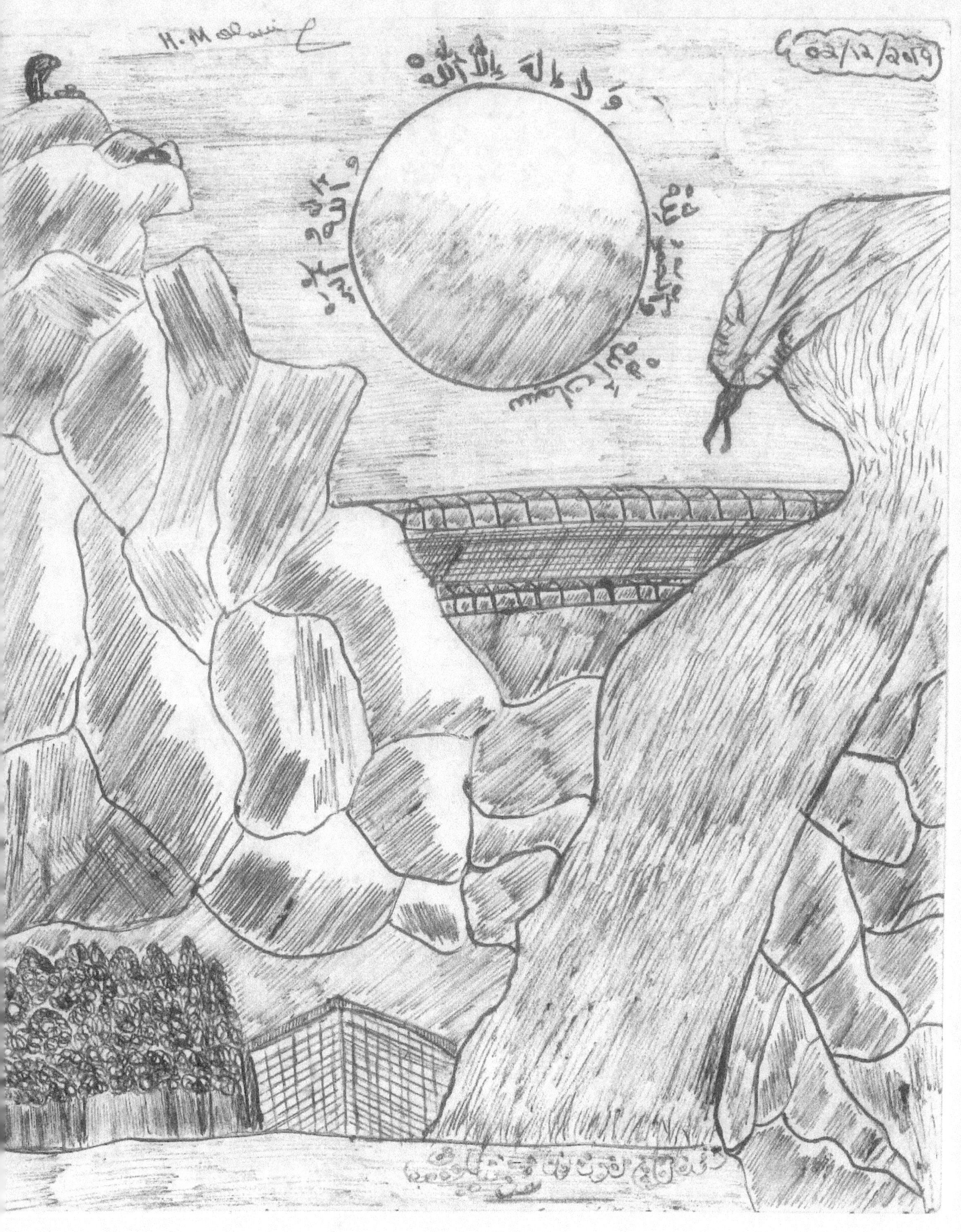

H. Moawi
03/12/2019
قل هو الله أحد

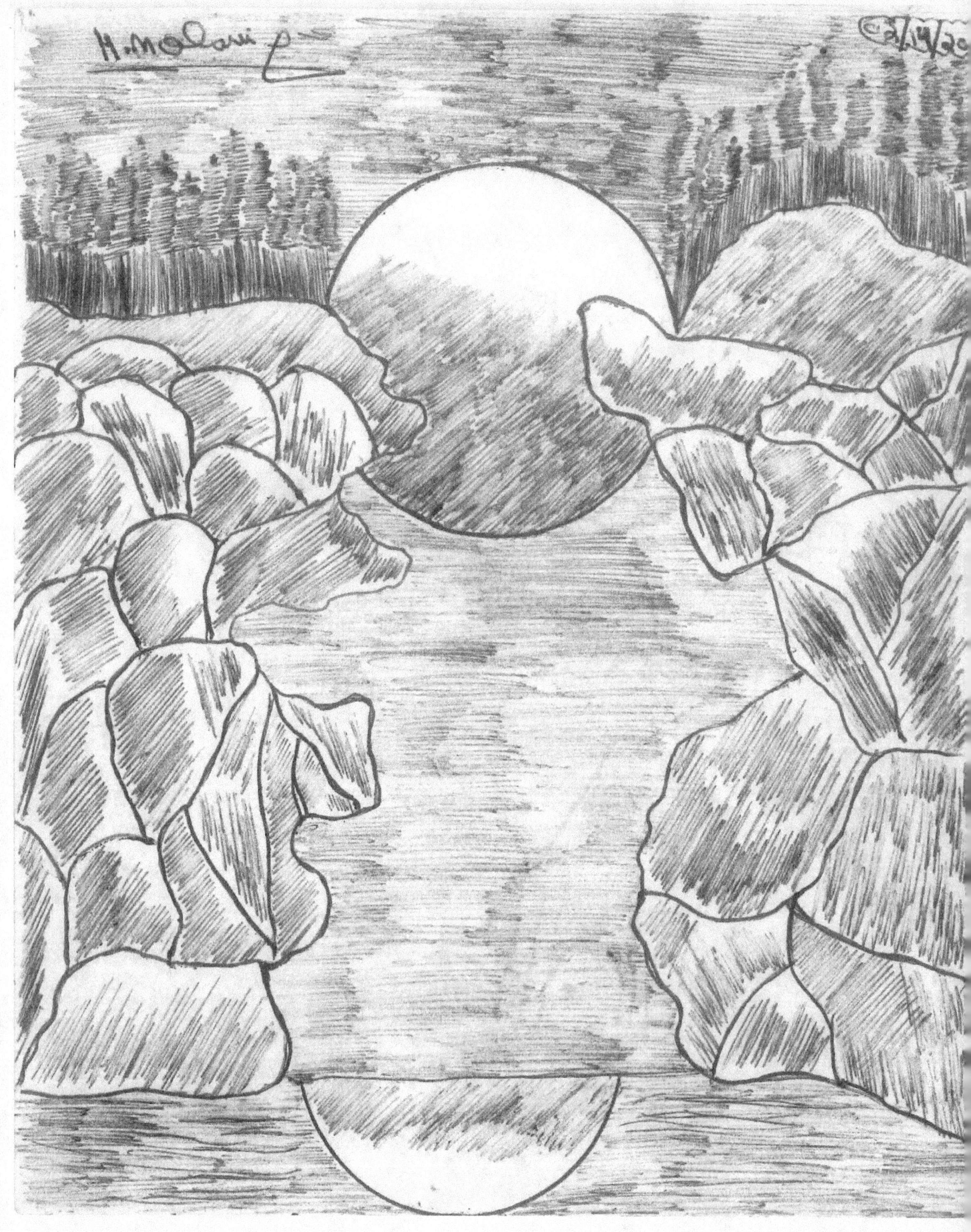

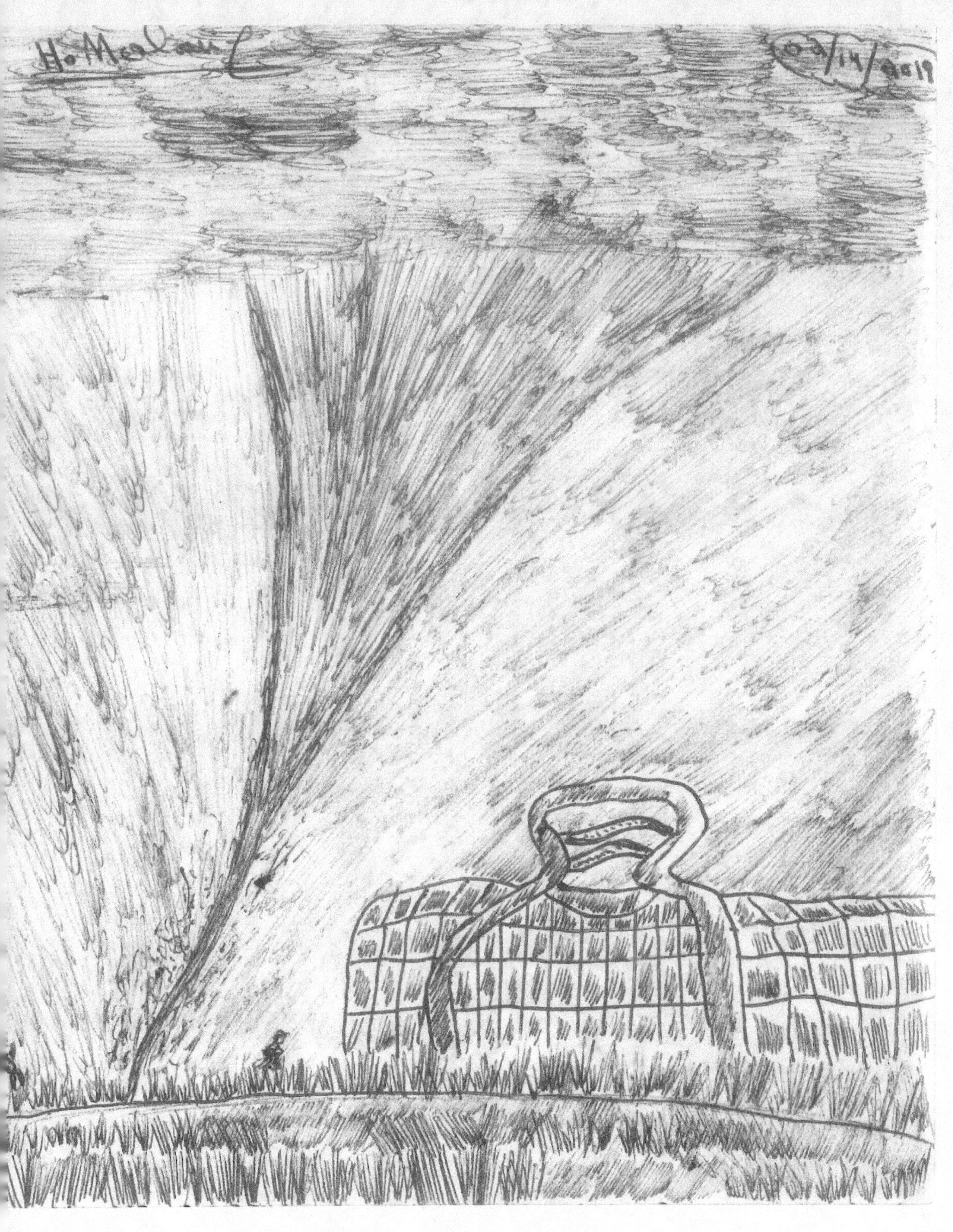

H. Meadow
03/14/2019

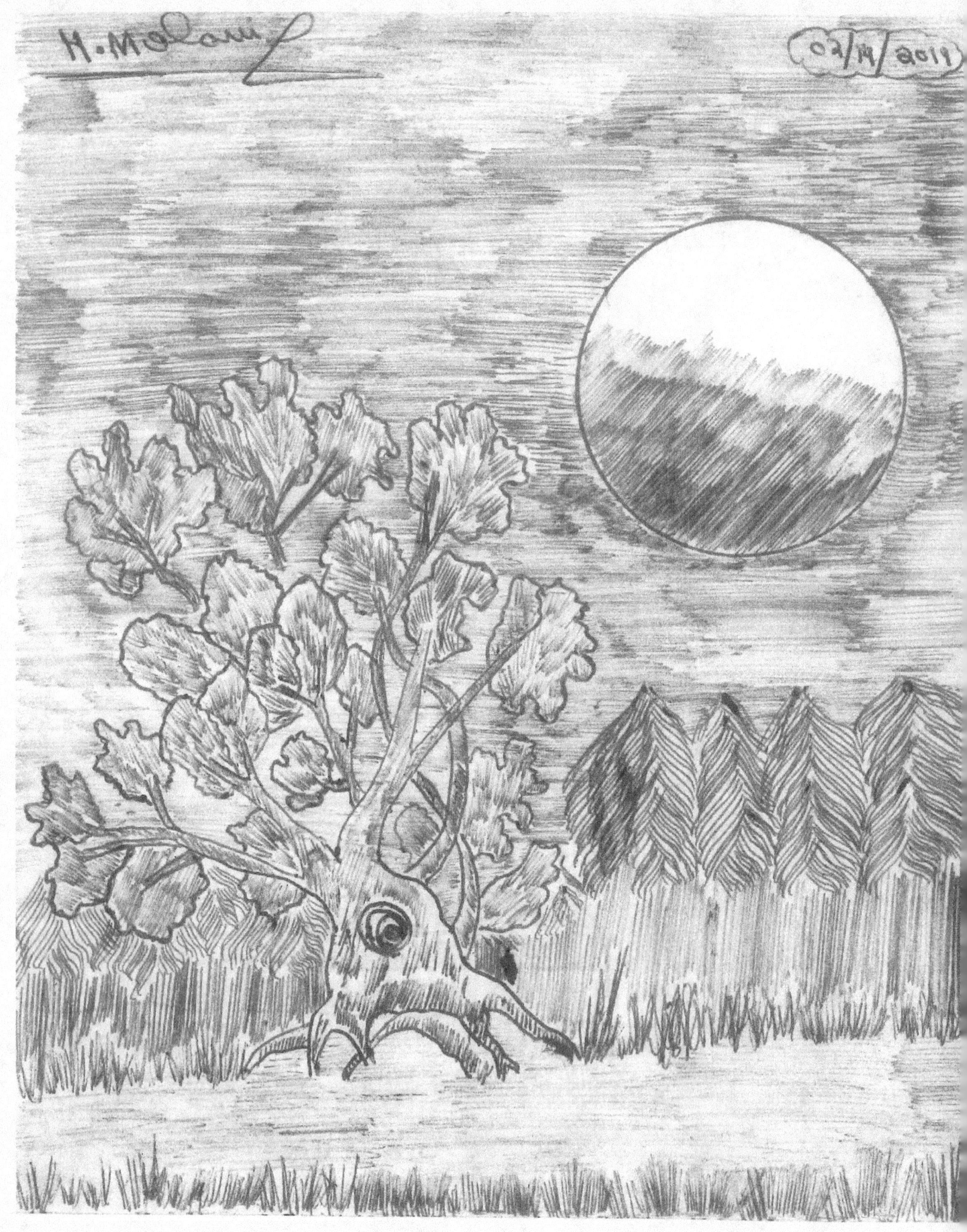

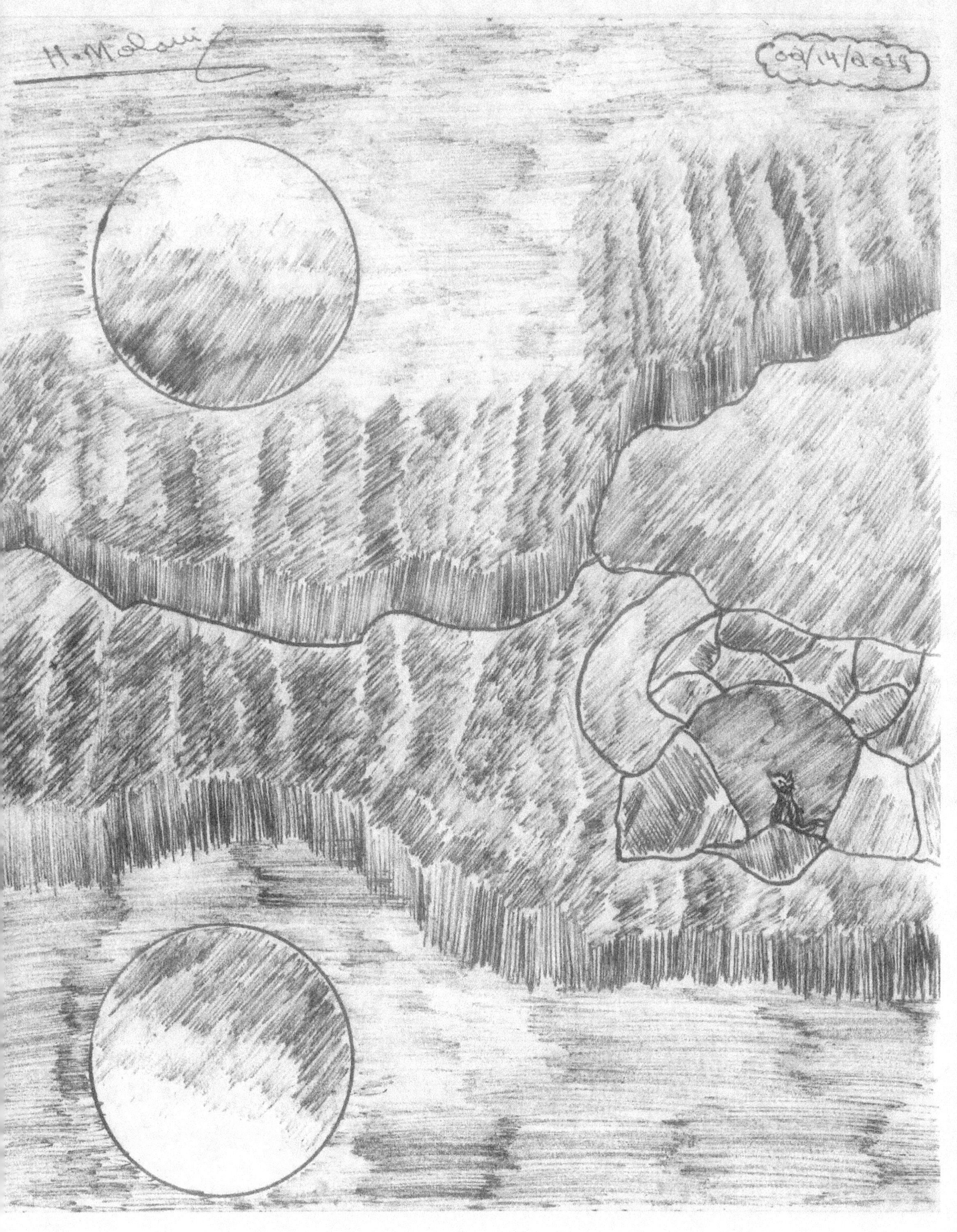

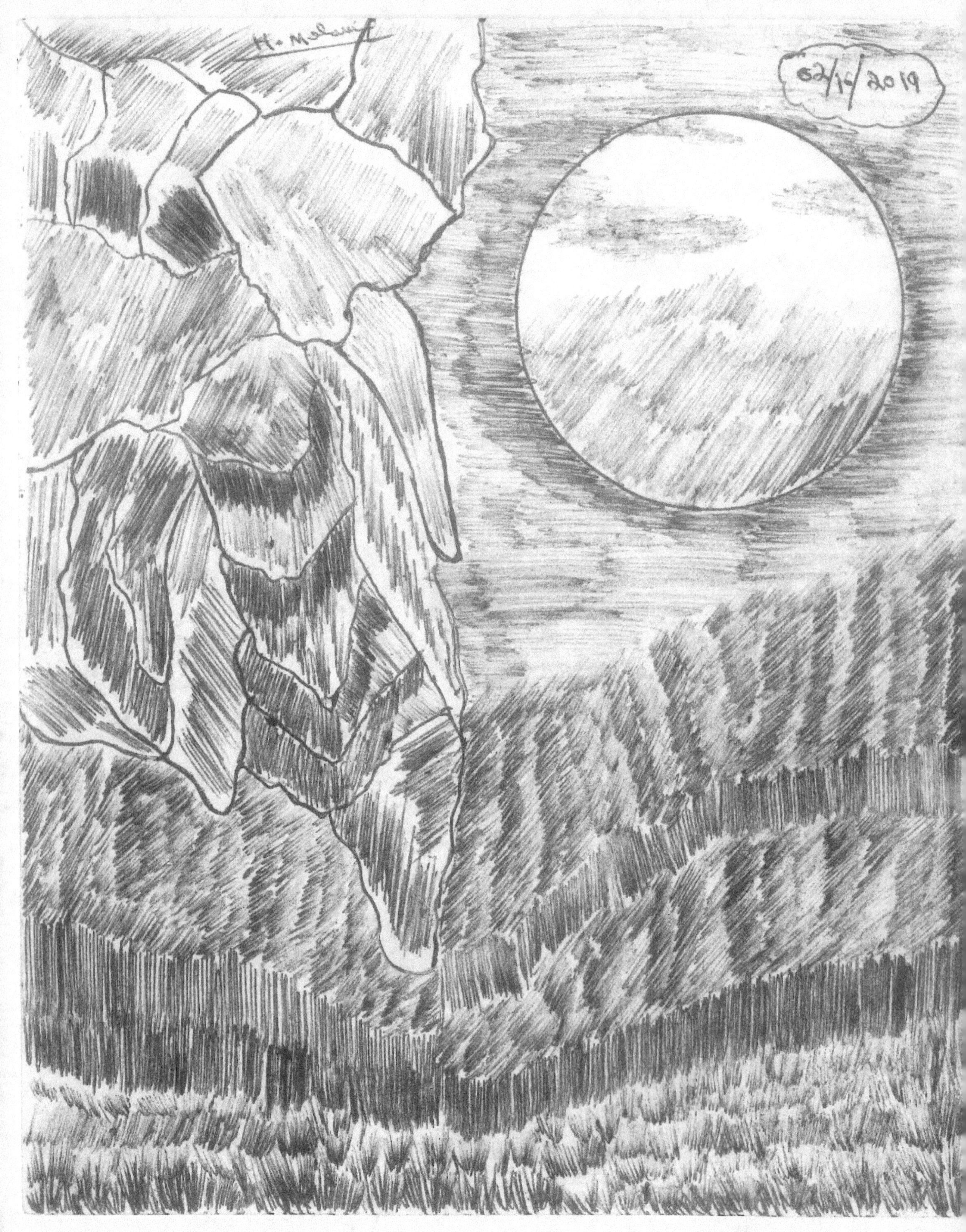
M. Melani
02/14/2019

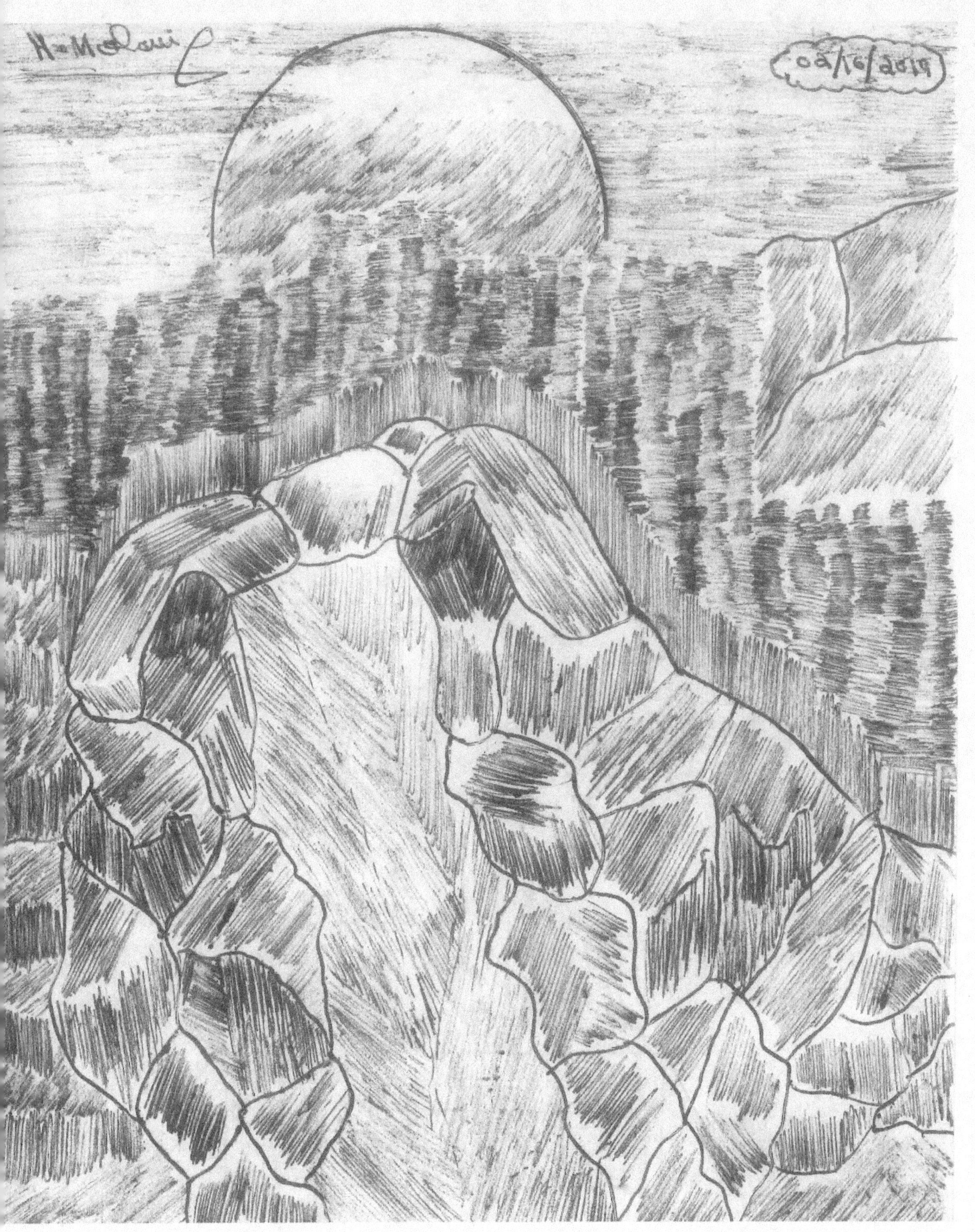

H.Mdaoui
02/16/2019

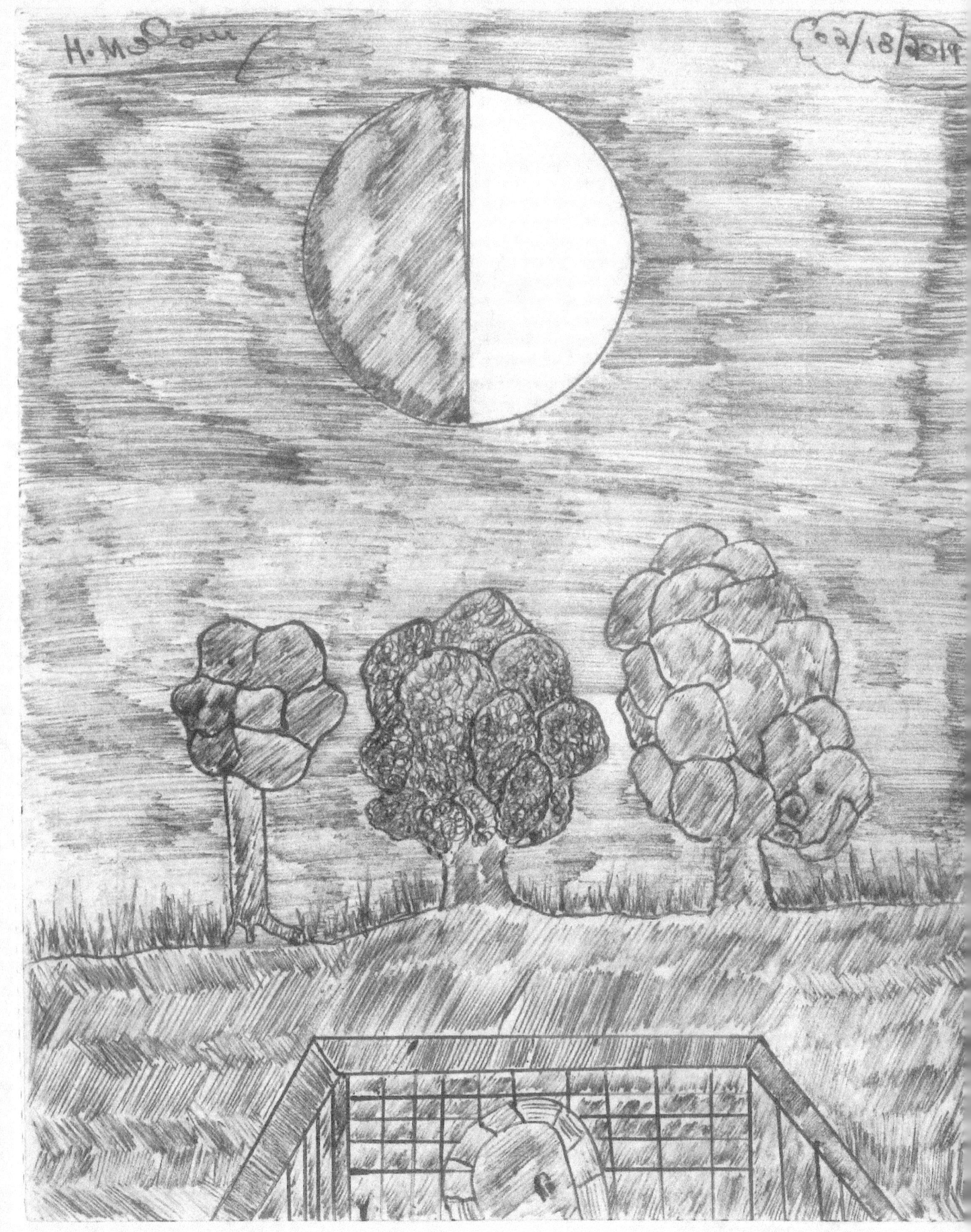
H.M.Qasim
02/18/2019

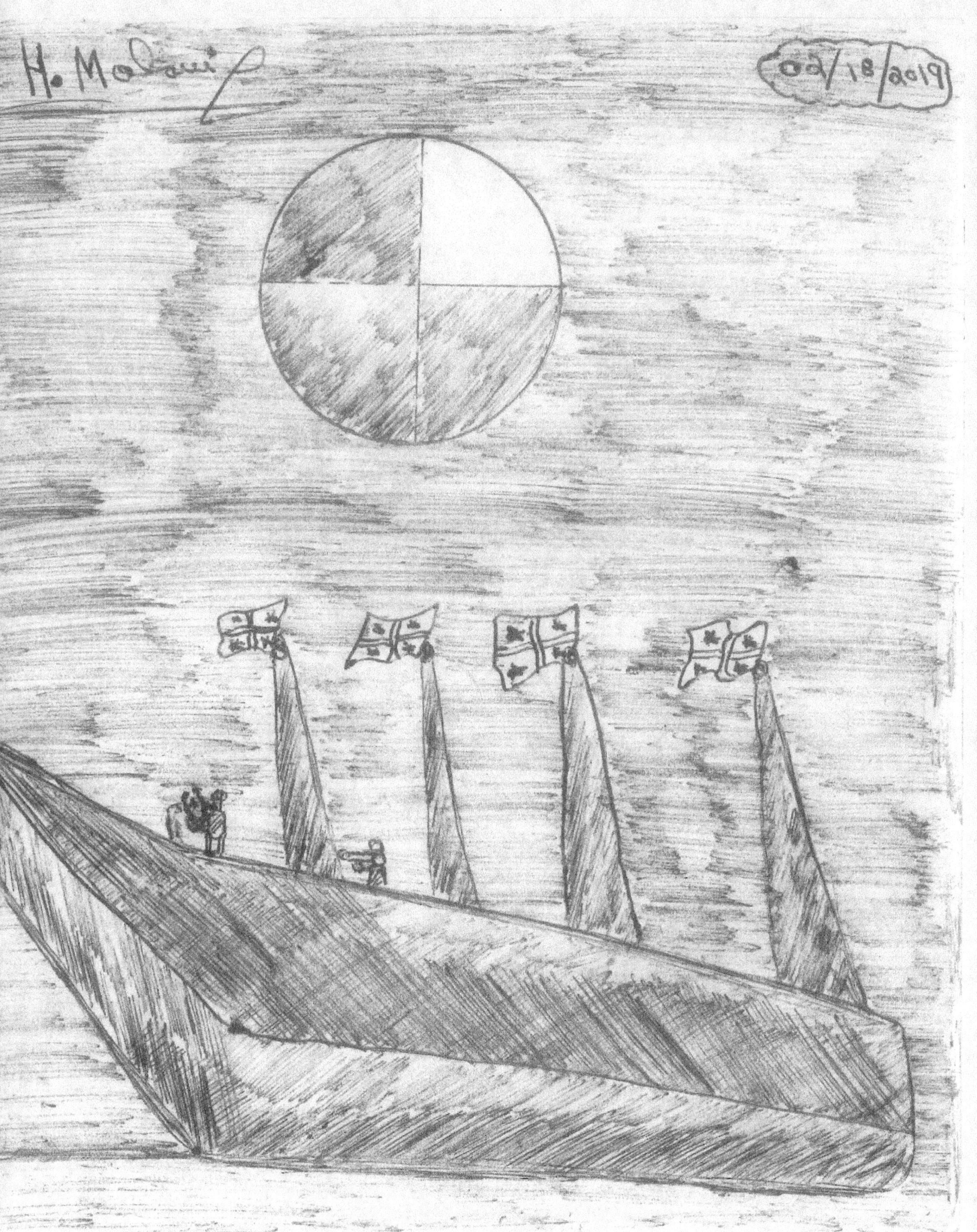

H. Moloui
02/18/2019

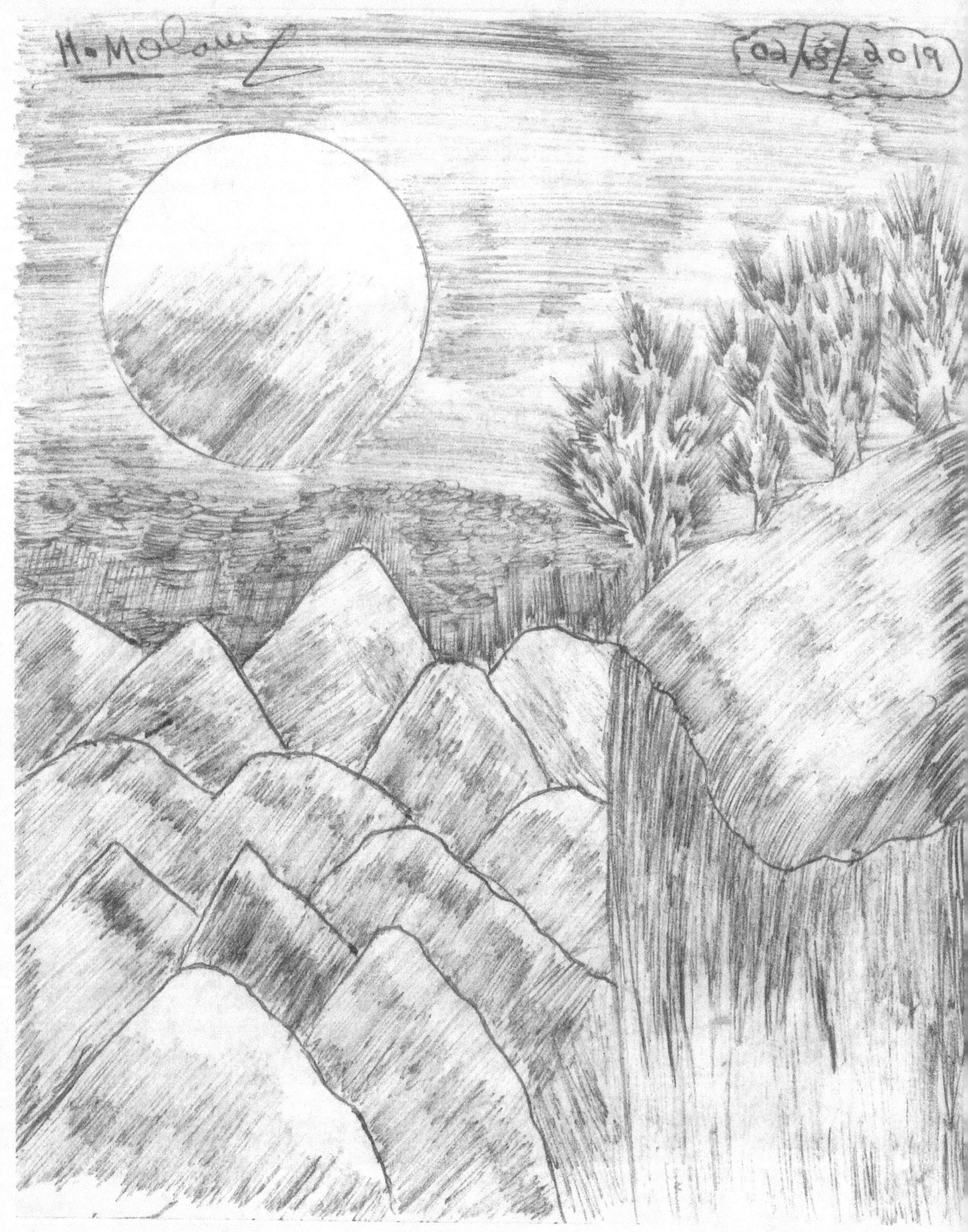

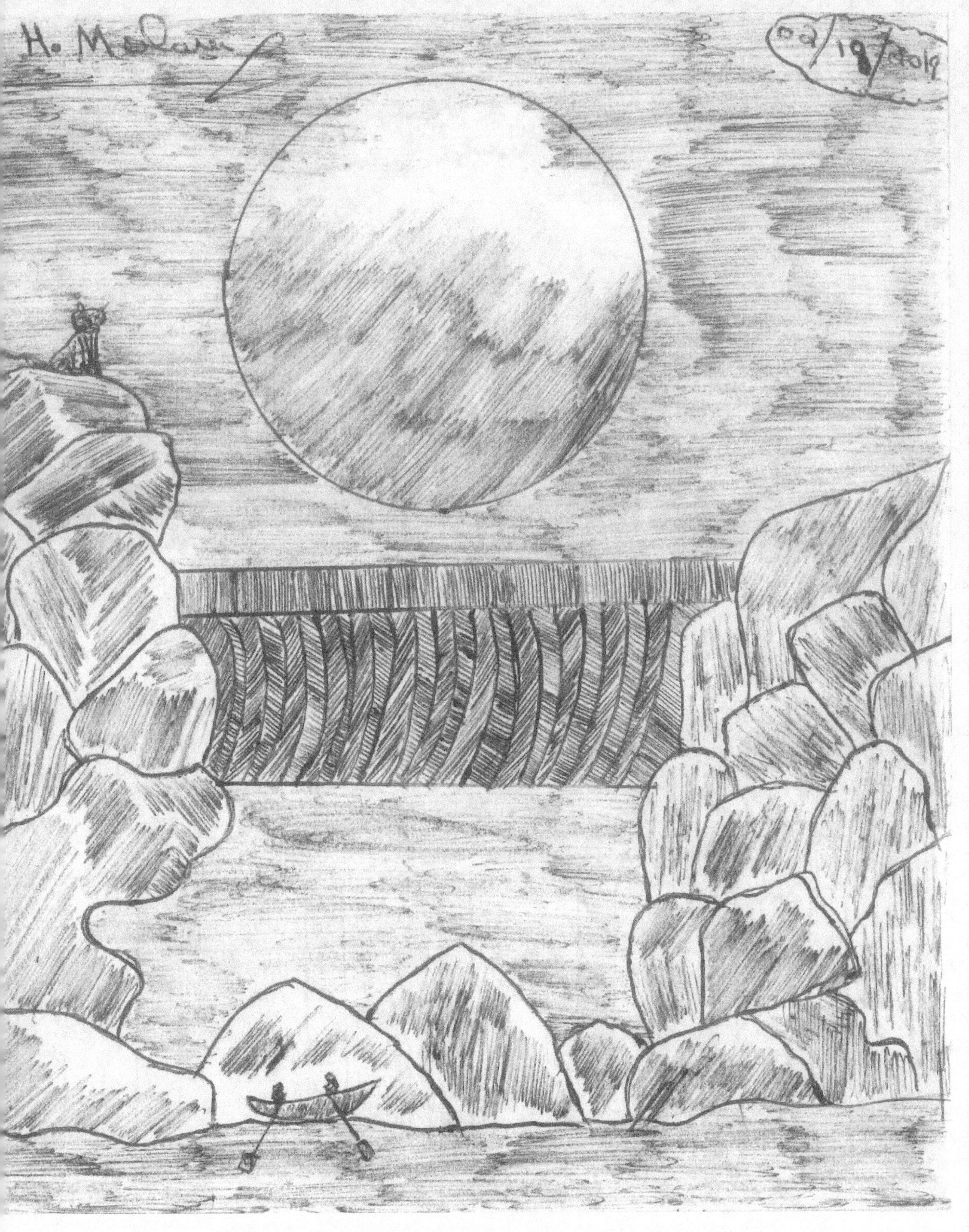

H. Molaw
02/19/2019

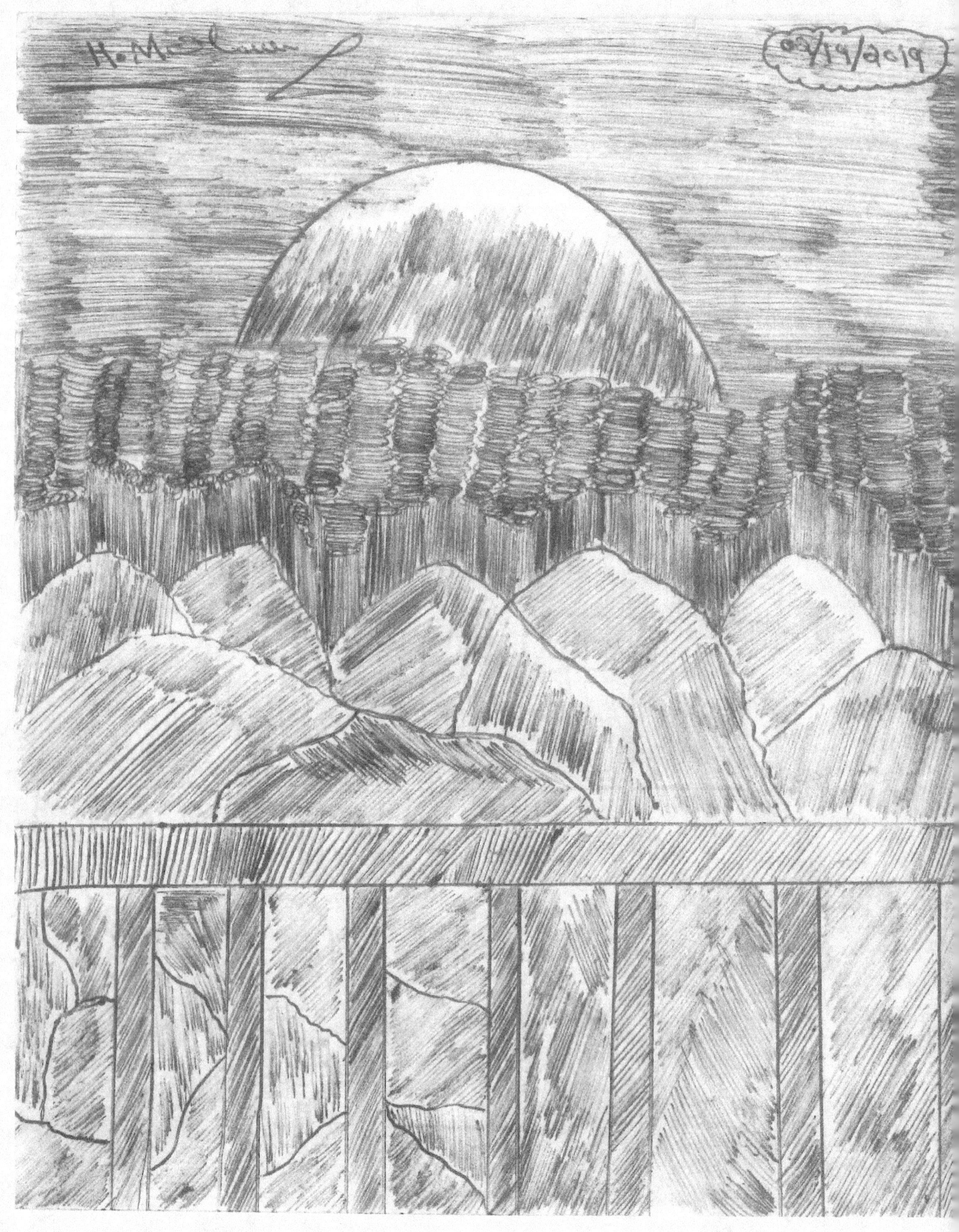

09/14/2019

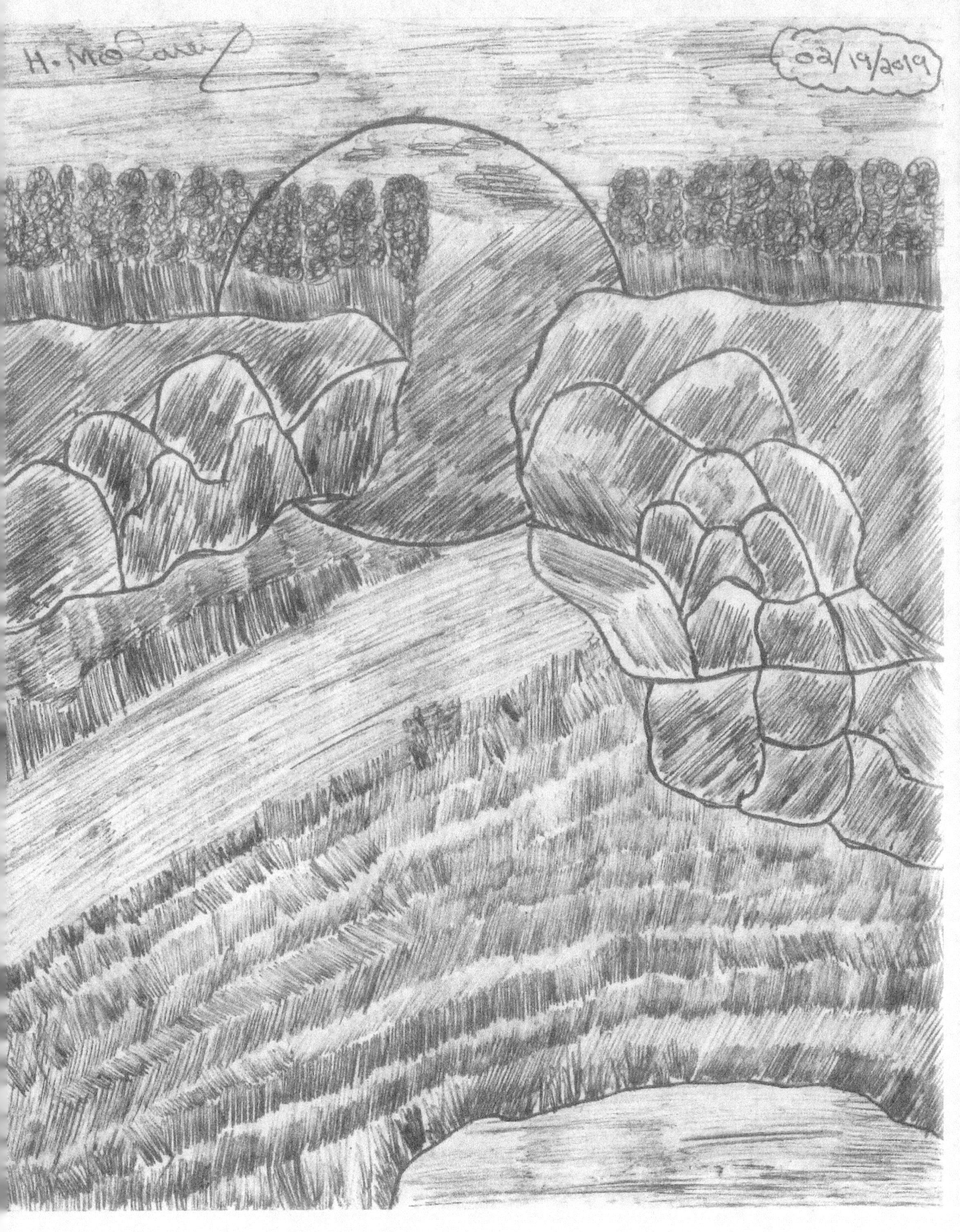

H. Mirzaei
02/19/2019

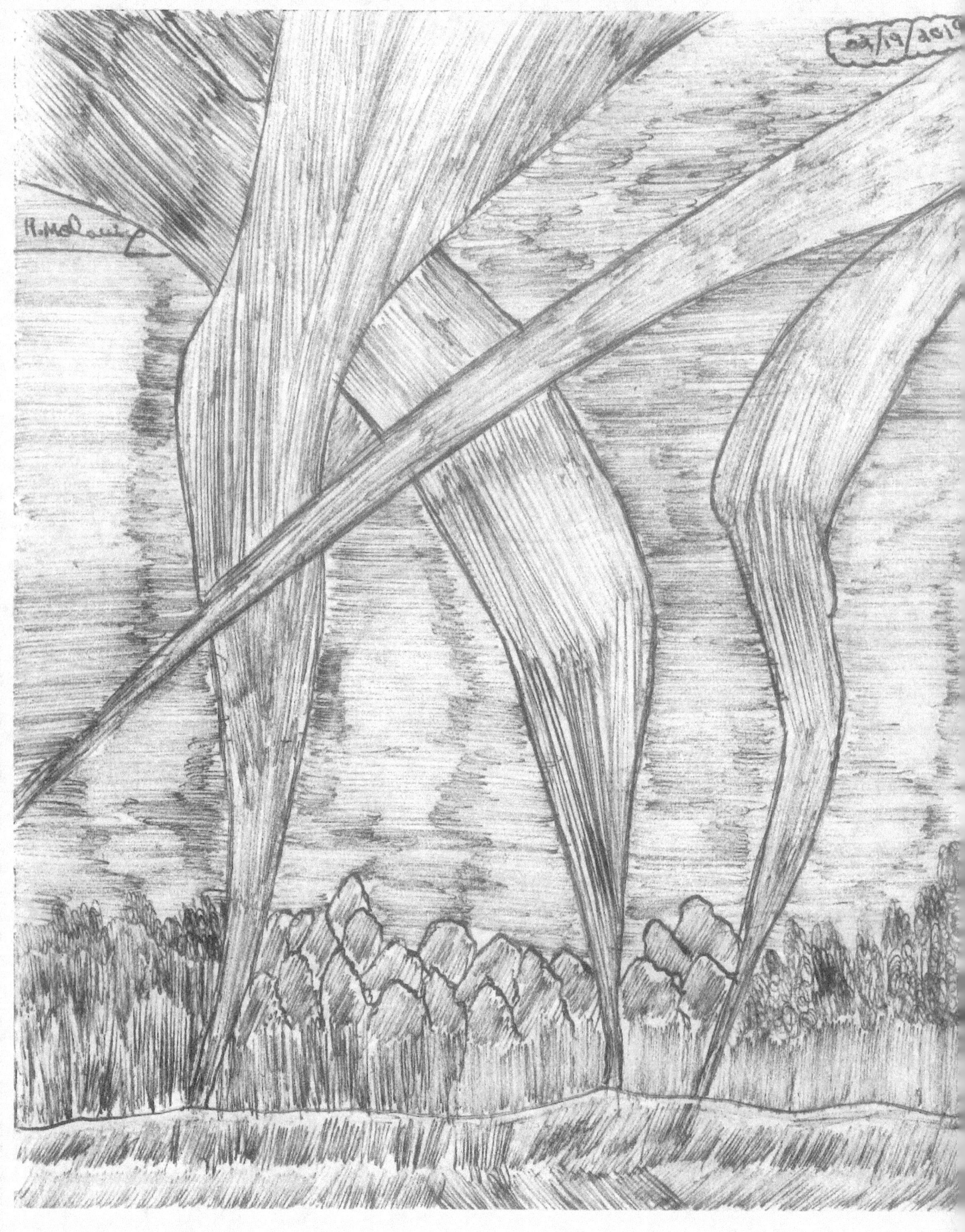

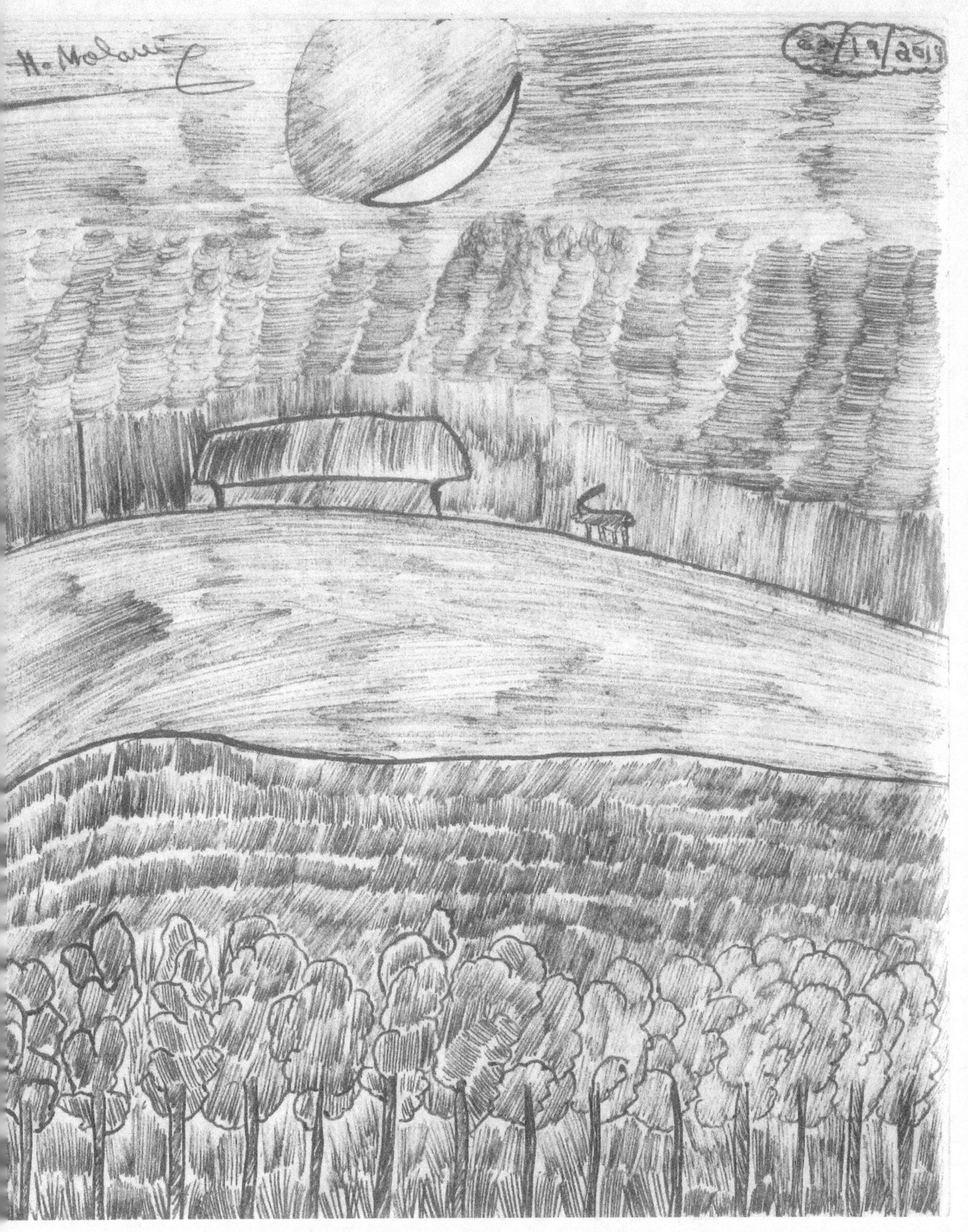
H. Molaei

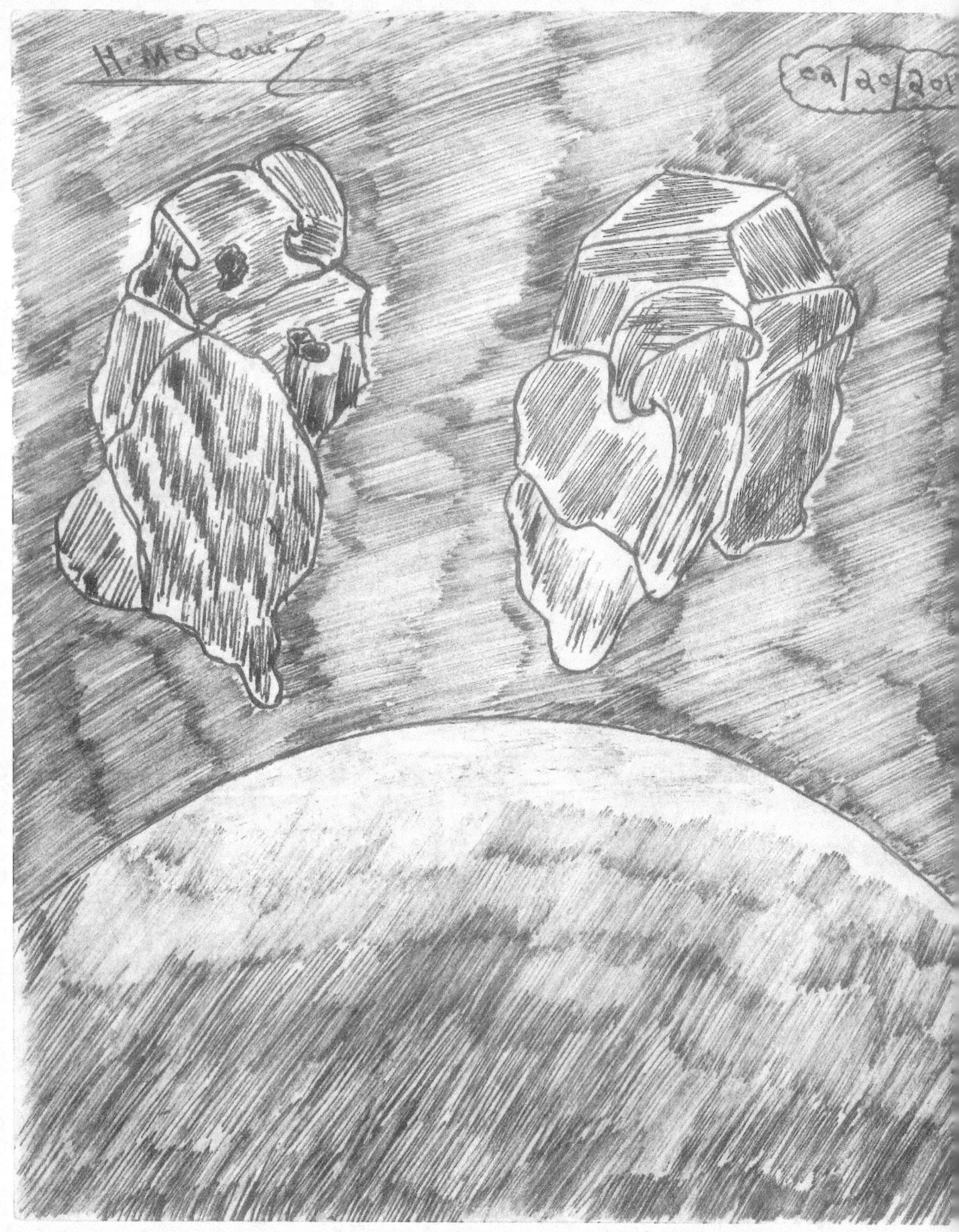

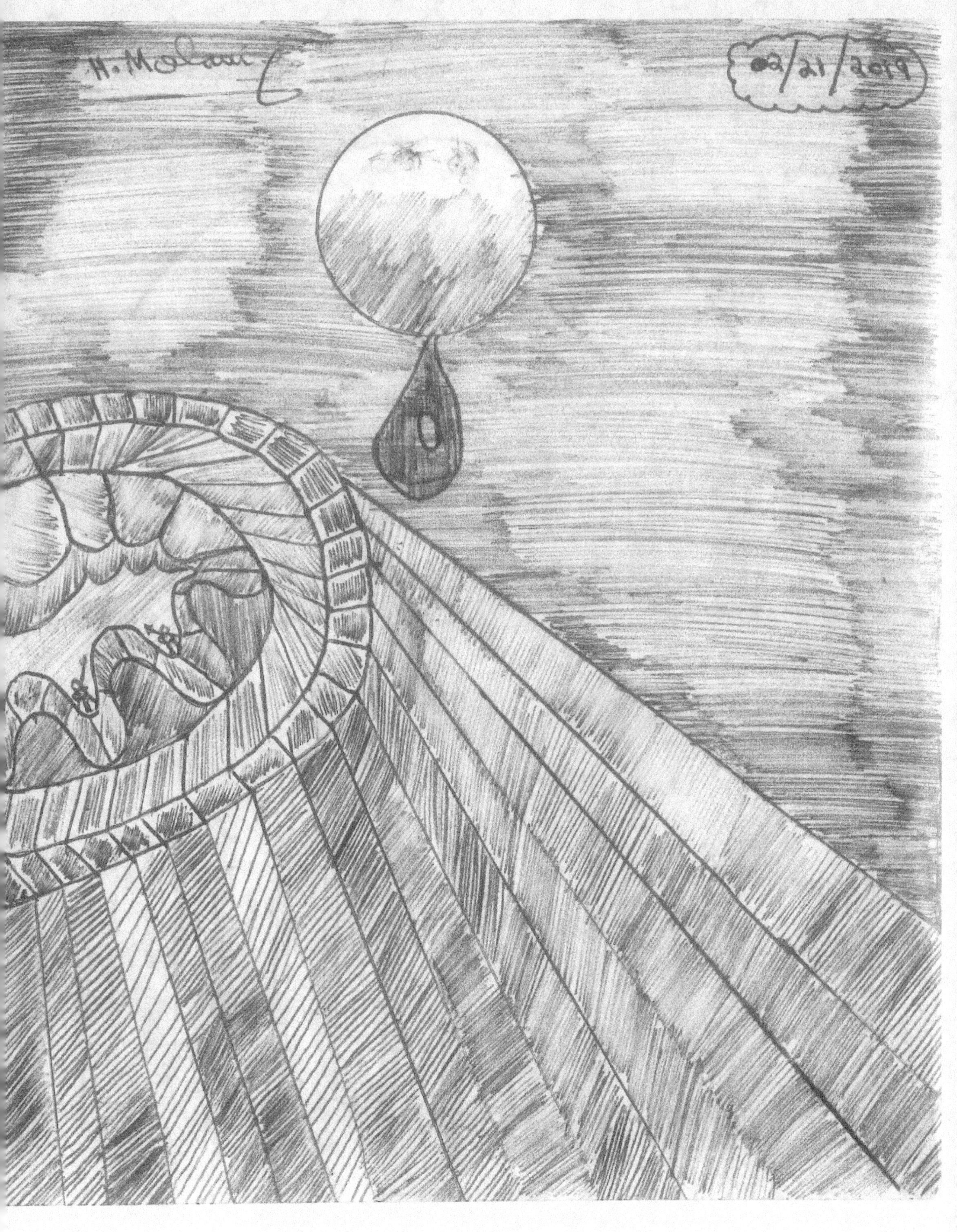

H. Molaei
2/21/2019

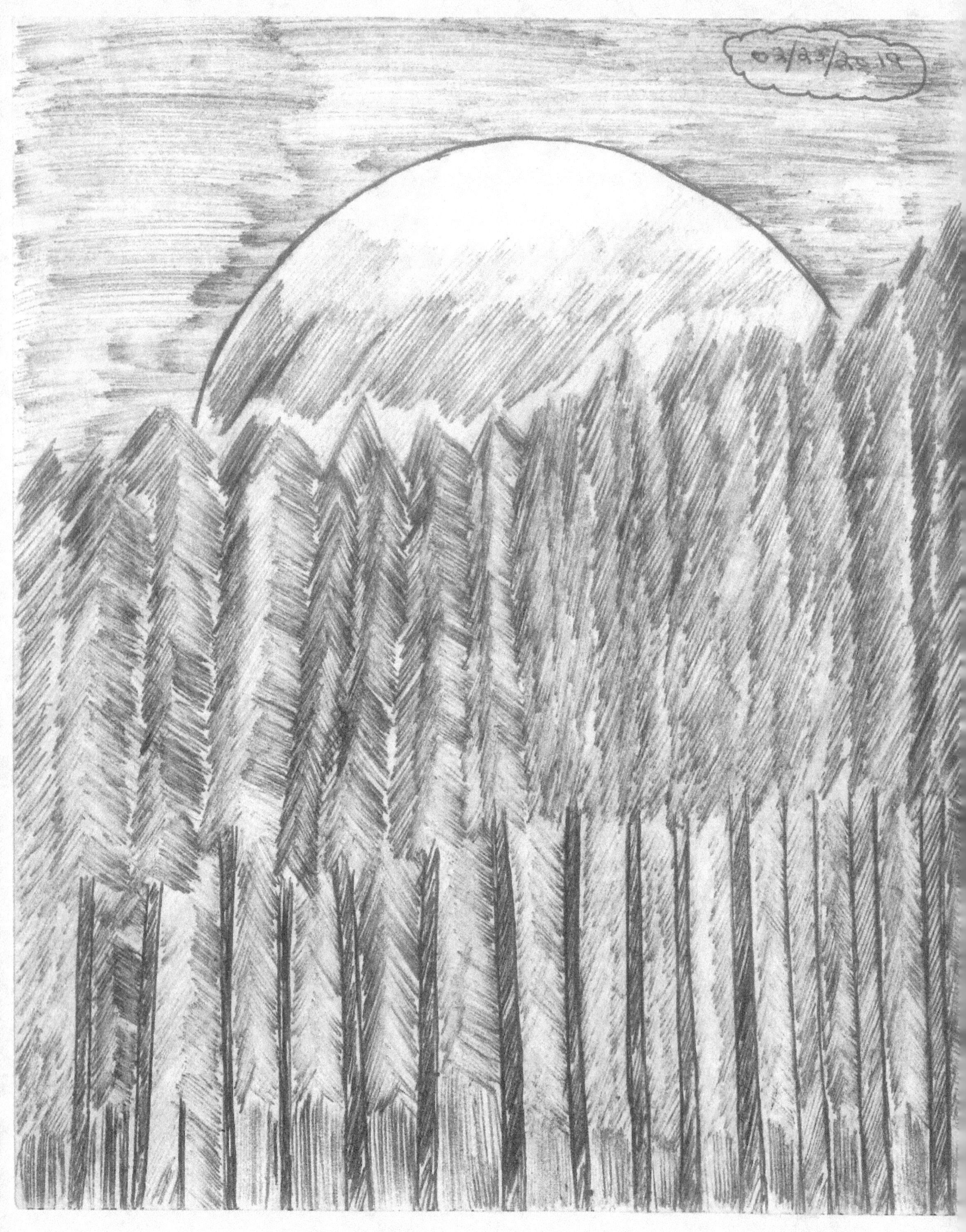
03/29/25.19

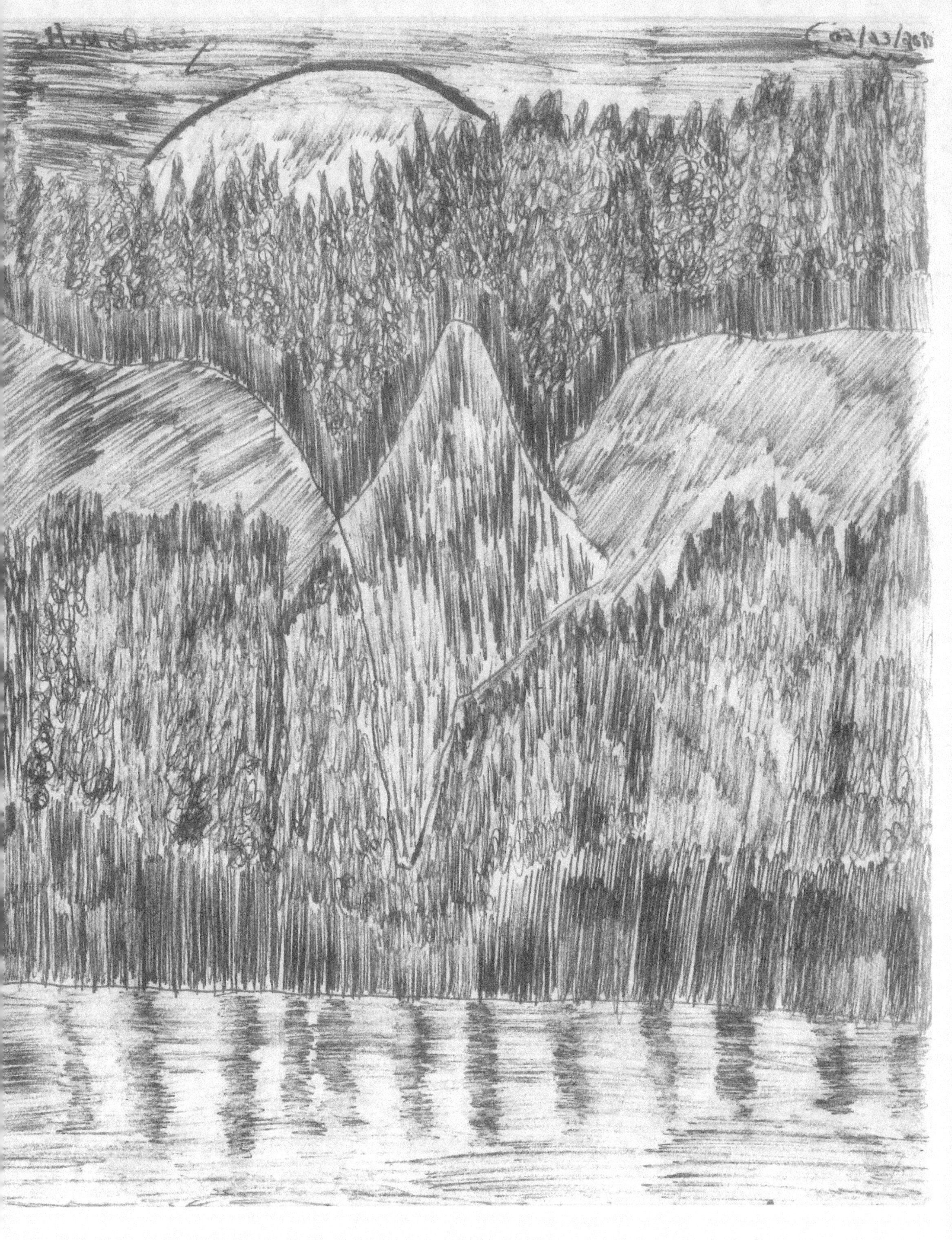

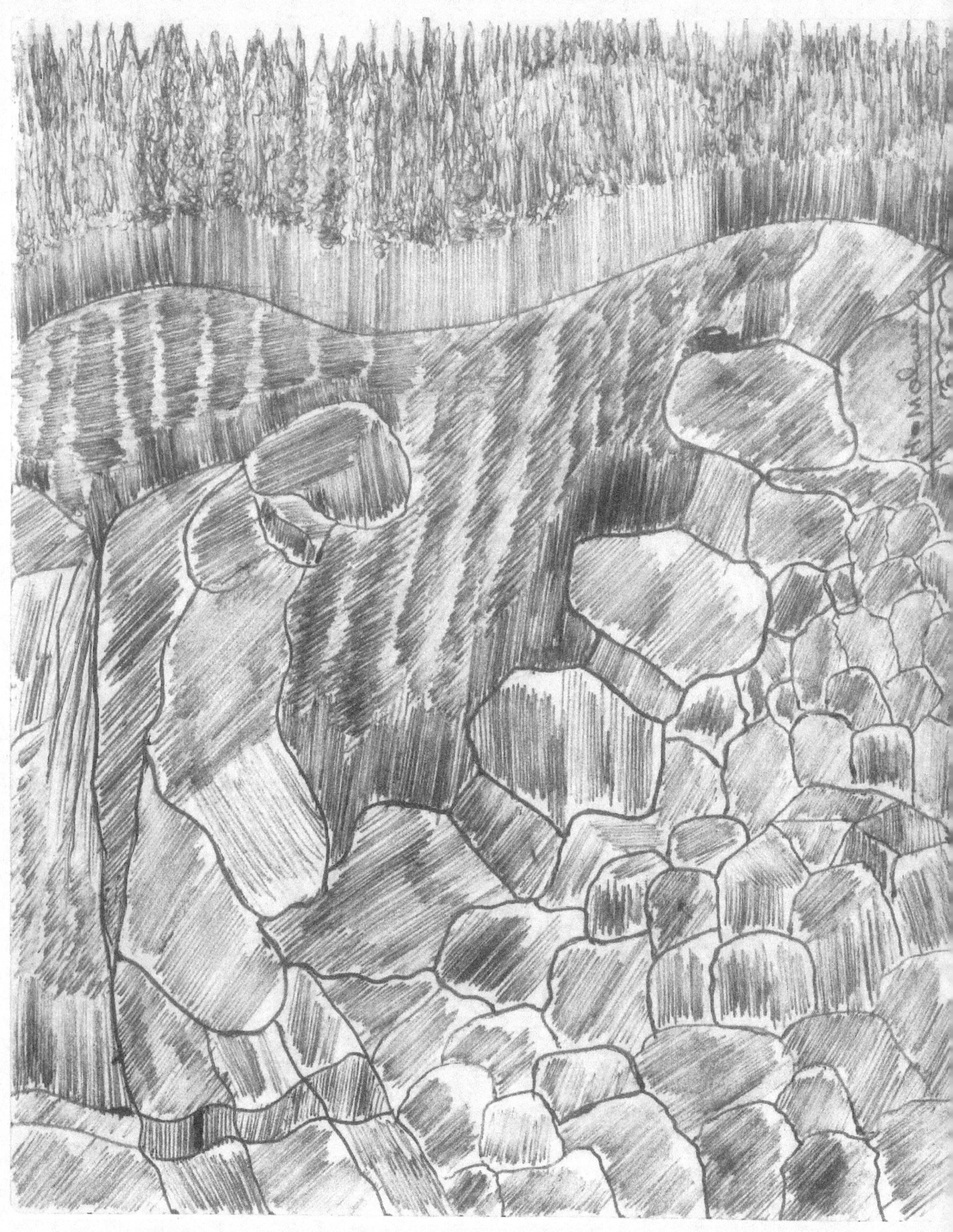

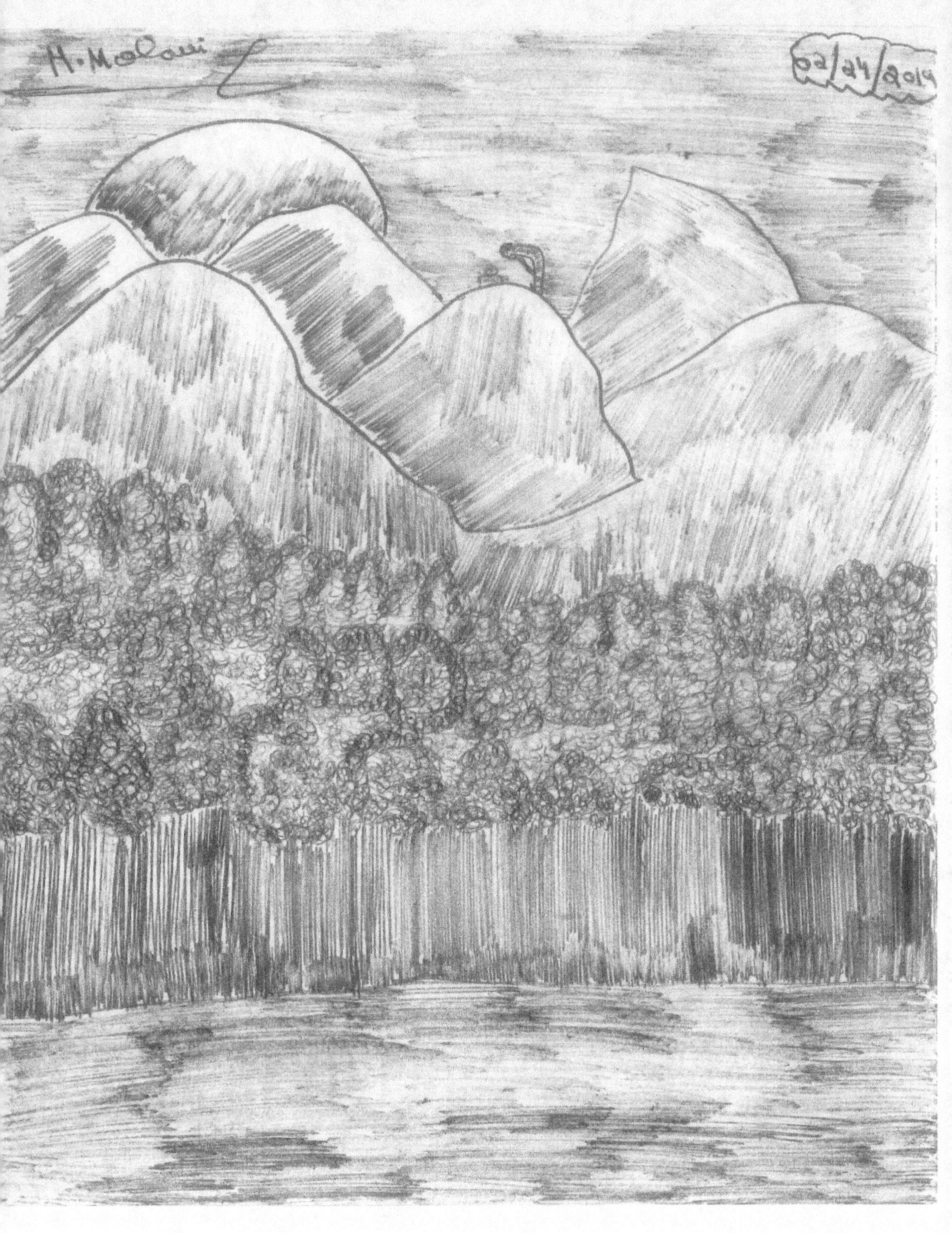

H. Molani
02/24/2019

ABOUT THE AUTHOR

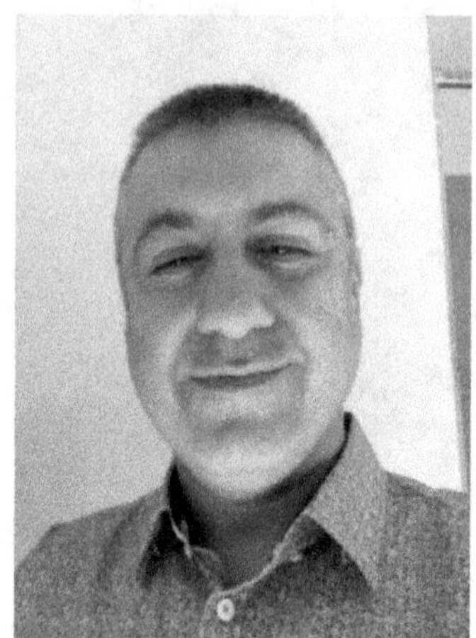

My name is Dr. Hamid Reza Molavi. I was born in 1969 in Tehran, Iran. My family immigrated to the USA in 1988. I am an immunologist/microbiologist as well as a pharmacist/artist. The almighty granted me the gift of drawing/sketching overnight and I have been developing my gift ever since. I play the flute, clarinet, and the Persian ney and hold a second-degree brown belt in Chinese kenpo

www.ingramcontent.com/pod-product-compliance
Lightning Source LLC
Chambersburg PA
CBHW081253250726
48654CB00012B/1590